Makarand Waingankar is one of India's most widely read cricket columnists, best known for blending meticulous research with his own experience of a life lived on the cricket fields of India. Journalist, columnist, researcher, talent-spotter and administrator, he wears a multitude of hats, each of which fits snugly on his head. He launched the Talent Resource Development Wing (TRDW) on behalf of the BCCI (Board of Control for Cricket in India) in 2002 and the TRDW has since been responsible for taking many small-town players to the national stage, including current India captain Mahendra Singh Dhoni. In fact, seven such players were part of the 2011 World Cup winning team. Makarand has also been CEO of Baroda Cricket Association and Consultant to Karnataka State Cricket Association's academy.

Yuvi

Makarand Waingankar

Harper
Sport

An Imprint of HarperCollins*Publishers*

First published in India in 2012 by Harper Sport
An imprint of HarperCollins *Publishers* India
a joint venture with
The India Today Group

Copyright © Makarand Waingankar 2012

ISBN: 978-93-5029-579-3

2 4 6 8 10 9 7 5 3 1

HarperCollins *Publishers*
A-53, Sector 57, Noida, Uttar Pradesh 201301, India
77-85 Fulham Palace Road, London W6 8JB, United Kingdom
Hazelton Lanes, 55 Avenue Road, Suite 2900, Toronto, Ontario M5R 3L2
and 1995 Markham Road, Scarborough, Ontario M1B 5M8, Canada
25 Ryde Road, Pymble, Sydney, NSW 2073, Australia
31 View Road, Glenfield, Auckland 10, New Zealand
10 East 53rd Street, New York NY 10022, USA

Typeset in 10.5/15 Meridien Lt Std
by Jojy Philip New Delhi 110 018

Printed and bound at
Thomson Press (India) Ltd.

This book is dedicated to Polly Umrigar and Frank Tyson, two men who gave back to cricket much more than they got from it.

Polly didn't have a mean bone in his huge frame and Frank had a heart of gold even while living up to his first name.

Mumbai and Indian cricket owe them a great deal. Me too.

CONTENTS

FOREWORD

I have known Yuvraj Singh's father Yograj since 1977, when we played in the Under-22 team against the touring MCC team led by Tony Greig.

Yograj was part of the late Col. Hemu Adhikari's camp that was held at the Cricket Club of India for many years under the auspices of the BCCI (Board of Control for Cricket in India). These camps had many young and upcoming cricketers, including the great Kapil Dev, Roger Binny and Yograj Singh himself. As a journalist, Makarand Waingankar used to write about these camps.

Once, Makarand's job took him to Jullundur; he was helping cricketers to get more exposure, especially those who came from the smaller states. He watched Yog at his practice and instantly thought, Here is a potential India player who must be encouraged.

Though Yog hadn't played any competitive cricket for a season, the national selectors, on Makarand's recommendation, picked him for the Board President's XI against Pakistan. The year was 1979. In the match at Baroda, Yog claimed three important wickets including those of Majid Khan and Javed Miandad.

Makarand took great interest in Yog's game and mentoring soon led to friendship. He got him down to Mumbai to play for Mafatlal in the prestigious Times Shield tournament. Yog got the exposure he needed as he played with and against Test and first-class players. Soon, he got picked for the 1980–81 tour of Australia, New Zealand and Fiji.

I got to know Yog very well on that tour and we became friends. In 1982, he invited me to Chandigarh along with Makarand and we spent about a week in the city which I was visiting for the first time. That was also the first time I saw Yuvi.

I visited Chandigarh many times during my playing career and each time discovered how much Yuvi had grown. He was scoring heavily in inter-state games. Though I did not see him play, word got around that here was a boy who would eventually play for India.

At their home, Yog showed me how he trained Yuvi in the backyard and told me that little Yuvi was finding it tough to cope with his hard-work mantra. I was surprised when he proudly pointed to a cupboard full of cricket bats he had bought for Yuvi.

One day, Yog called me from Chandigarh to say that he wanted to send Yuvi to my cricket academy in Mumbai. He felt Mumbai would offer tougher lessons to Yuvi and he would make better progress as a cricketer. I was happy to include Yuvi in the set-up. As he was staying with Makarand at Andheri, a suburb in Mumbai, he had to take a train to come to Churchgate where my academy is located.

The first day was a nightmare for young Yuvi as he found travelling in a crowded local train extremely difficult. However, he got used to it and became a regular member of the team. I sent him with the academy team to Satara, in southern Maharashtra, in the summer and he not only performed with the bat but also fielded brilliantly on a bouncy outfield. One could see the talent in him as he cleared the ground time and again with remarkable ease. He certainly was a special talent.

In later years, Yuvi played first-class cricket for Punjab and scored heavily. His India debut was on the cards and soon, he was picked for the 2000 Champions Trophy in Nairobi.

India had a strong and settled middle order then and Yuvi had to wait for his Test opportunity. I was in Lahore in 2004 – all the former Test captains had been invited to watch the match – when Yuvi scored a brilliant hundred. After watching him bat, I thought he would play Test cricket for many years for India.

Unfortunately, he was not given enough opportunities to settle down in the squad and had the sword hanging over his head each time he went in to bat. This helped neither Yuvi nor the team.

When I became the chairman of the selection committee in 2006, Yuvi was included in the playing XI against Pakistan. And what a century he scored in the last Test match at Bangalore! It was an innings right out of the top drawer.

However, just before the 2007 World Cup, he twisted his knee and was sidelined for most of the season. That was a big blow to his career. He fought hard, came back into the team, did very well in the one-dayers and T20s but could not get going in Test cricket. Surprisingly, he found the short stuff difficult to handle, and that's where he continued to struggle despite being enormously talented.

Yuvi is a fighter, as is evident from his struggle against cancer. In comparison, I am sure, overcoming his weakness against short-pitched deliveries will be very easy for him.

He just has to apply his mind and then I am sure we will see Yuvi the world beater once again.

Finally, a word about the author of this unusual book: Makarand Waingankar is passionate about the game at all levels and is a very good and experienced writer. His views on the game, its administration and players have always been forthright. He has also been a very close family friend of Yuvi and his understanding of the young man and his unique circumstances is one of the many reasons why you will enjoy reading this book.

DILIP VENGSARKAR
September 2012

Introduction

My journey as a cricket journalist dates back to 1969. I covered matches and wrote columns for national newspapers but never thought of writing a book. Many urged me to write, explaining that experience is useless if not shared. When I refused to succumb to the pressure, one of them said that I didn't have it in me to write a book.

That hurt, because to me, cricket is a way of life. For more than four decades, I have been following the progress of Indian cricket. And it was the 'why' factor in the sport that motivated me to initiate various cricket projects, including this book.

Having been responsible, among other things, for the Talent Resource Wing for the BCCI which helps to unearth players from the small towns of India, I have come to the conclusion that a cricketer's success has much do with the circumstances of his life and how he responds to these. One of the worst things to happen to a child, perhaps, is to be born with a gigantic middle name, a name that is keen to ensure that his son achieves what he couldn't. While the great Don Bradman's son changed his name to Bradson, Philip, son of 'Typhoon' Frank Tyson, gave up the game when he was called 'breeze' for bowling medium pace.

The extent to which parents will go to make something of their kid is bizarre. I was witness to one such experiment in Sector 11, in the city of Chandigarh, the home of former Indian cricketer Yograj Singh. There must be many ways for a man to encourage his son to become a cricketer, but the methods adopted by this father were unique, closest perhaps to what Andre Agassi underwent to become a superstar.

Even more unique was the conviction in the man. He had absolute faith that he would win the battle he was preparing his son for. The father was determined, but what about the boy whose life was being scripted without his consent?

He had a strange childhood. Did he understand why he couldn't do the things his friends did? Did he understand why he was the only child in the world who was being treated this way? The game of cricket was torture for him; it's a miracle that he didn't break down at some point.

No amount of reasoning on my part could dissuade Yograj Singh from his chosen path. His explanation was simple: 'What I couldn't achieve after working like a donkey, I will get my son to achieve.' From then on, my visits to his house were mute. Yuvi's mother Shabnam, herself a state basketball player, had no say in the matter and however much Yog's old mother muttered about his methods, her voice was never heeded. Nothing could change Yograj Singh. He listened to only one thing: the voice of his past, which had experienced – and hated – failure.

Once, I saw the kid, then eleven years of age, weep after being hit by a hard ball during a makeshift backyard practice session in the severe winter of Chandigarh. I was furious. I could not bear to see it anymore. The boy's misery increased day by day. However, as he grew, things began to fall into place. I was surprised, but Yograj wasn't. His plan was working. There was a method in the madness after all.

Yuvraj Singh, as we know him today, is the product of that method of madness. I have watched every step of his journey. I did not approve of the method, no one did. But it did work.

One morning in December 2011, I got a call from Karthika V.K., Publisher and Chief Editor of HarperCollins India. She requested me to write a book on Yuvi. My immediate reaction was, 'why not?' but the evening brought with it a set of dilemmas. How could I describe what I had observed? Could moments like these be translated into words?

I was distraught. Maybe that person who had said to me that I couldn't ever write a book was right after all. Then Karthika came to Mumbai to meet me and after talking to her, everything started to make sense. She said to me: 'You have known Yuvraj from his younger days, you are the right person to write this book.'

Engrossed in my PhD thesis on the history of Mumbai cricket, I had thought writing a book on Yuvi would drain me out, partly because I knew more than anyone else did. But Karthika gave me confidence. I began to feel that it was my duty, perhaps, to write the book. What I had seen should be documented. Stories get lost if not told, and this story should not be lost. For at the heart of this tale is a dilemma that every reader has faced, or is likely to. Was Yograj Singh right in doing what he did? Is Yuvraj Singh the cricketer a compensation, a justification for what his father underwent?

There is something of Yograj in every one of us. We all see ourselves in our children, invest our own dreams in them, burden them with our unfulfilled ambitions. To question Yograj is to question ourselves. What does your child mean to you? Is your child living out a prophecy that you outlined for him/her? Is your child leading his life or yours?

This book was a personal journey for me, a revisiting not only of the past but of everything that happened around me. As more and more youngsters join national teams as teenagers, the pursuit of stardom goes on. Around me are kids who want to become famous cricketers and parents who want their children to become superstars.

The goal is lustrous, but what of the means? Is stardom worth the turmoil? What often becomes more important than the tale itself is the way it is told. How could I put a lifetime of experience onto paper? To dig into the past was to dig into memories. Memories that have been distorted by success.

I must confess I spent sleepless nights thinking about how to weave together all the different strands. Here I must state that I was helped a great deal by Shireen Azam, the twenty-year-old daughter of my friend Mohammad Azam. I was worried that my personal biases would affect how I looked back on events, but Shireen helped me edit the manuscript like a true professional.

When you see someone grow, you develop a unique bond with them. Yuvi, to me, is not just the man the world sees him as. In him I will always see the infant Yuvi, the child, the teenager, the man trying to make a mark in the world. At the same time, this book is not only about one man called Yuvraj Singh. It is about many Yuvrajs. I have tried to present the other side of the entertainer. I hope I have succeeded in my attempt.

MAKARAND WAINGANKAR

September 2012

Chapter One

CHASING THE DREAM

The hall is dark except for the spotlight which follows the dancer as she walks onto the stage. The musician enters right after her and takes up his position at the other end. He begins to play, slowly.

The dancer's body starts to sway to the music, not a finger out of sync. The music plays smoothly, not a note out of place. The musician plays like magic, and the dancer dances like a dream. The music increases in tempo and intensity, and so does the dancer's body, moving almost effortlessly. They go on in unison, reaching a crescendo, then they finally stop. The performance ends. They take a bow. The lights come on. A hundred chairs stare at the dancer and the musician. The hall is empty.

By definition the word 'perform' means to enact or present a piece for an audience. The performance is meaningless unless there is someone to appreciate it.

It is the audience that looks upon performers with awe, wonder and reverence. We are enthralled by their talent. We call ourselves their fans. We love them. We are intrigued by them. We want to know everything about their personal lives – their habits, likes, dislikes, interests, affairs, secrets. They become an obsession almost and we go to any length to meet them, to get their autograph, a souvenir, a memento – anything related to them. We chase them, we keep chasing them.

But who are we chasing? Is it the person or the performer? We create a star out of a performer. And often, in this relationship between the performer and the audience, the person inside the performer gets lost.

We pay little heed to the talent, the inherent skill, and focus only on the entertainment quotient of the act. Talent or skill is irrelevant unless it is of 'use' to the audience. So we become 'fans' only of those who have the capacity to fulfil our need to be entertained.

Thus we reduce the performer to a mere entertainer. He becomes a slave to the expectations of the masses and is dependent on them, for fame, for money, for appreciation, for his very survival. And we, the audience, become more and more demanding. He continues to do everything that is demanded of him until he reaches a point where he has nothing left to give.

It doesn't matter what the activity is. Life treats a dancer, singer, actor and sportsman in much the same way.

On the day when a match is being played, the television is left on in many offices. Every now and then, people get up to check the score. If India is playing well, they linger for five minutes; if India is playing badly, they make faces, crack a joke and get back to their work. If they see that an Indian is batting on 90, they call everyone to see him get his century. If they find him batting on 70, they watch a few balls being played, yawn and return to their desks.

Unless, of course, it's someone like Yuvraj Singh at the crease. Someone who is known to be an entertainer.

'Oh my god! Three sixes in three balls! Come on, come quickly, Yuvraj is belting Stuart Broad. Three sixes in three balls already. Oh, you missed Yuvraj and Flintoff's fight in the last over. Ha ha, this is so awesome. Woah! Another six! Is this for real!'

The whole office gathers in front of the TV. From the peon to the boss, everyone stands with bated breath, staring at the screen, biting their nails. It is the last ball of the over. Broad is running in and everyone's heart is in their mouth.

SIX!

Everyone is screaming. The whole office is on fire. Jumping, hugging, dancing. It's a carnival. They can't believe it. There's only one name on their lips: Yuvraj Singh!

They are following every ball of the match now. It's a close match. . . When India finally wins, they rejoice. They are proud of their team. Proud of being Indian. Proud of the game of cricket which runs in India's veins, their veins.

But what happens when the Indian team doesn't perform so well? How many of us care to stand in front of the TV then? How many appreciate a painstaking 60 runs made on a tough wicket? We dismiss the team as a bunch of losers not worth wasting time over.

Despite the claims we make about our love for the game, the reverence for it, cricket is only a game for us. Our mood may be temporarily affected by an India win or loss, but our lives and jobs don't depend on it. And we enjoy a strange love–hate relationship with those who play the game. When they are successful we applaud their performance, we heap praise on them. But when they fail, we insult them, we call them traitors and mercenaries who lack pride and commitment. We burn their effigies and stone their houses.

Why do we do this? Is it for them? Or is it for ourselves? Is national pride and patriotism embodied in the performance of the men in blue? Do they become the symbols through which we, the citizen–fans, express our patriotism?

When the player on view falls while playing a match, we curse him for being careless. But if he gets injured before or after a match, we pray for him to get well soon and to get back into the team. Do we really care about the player?

For the man in blue playing on the small TV in the shopkeeper's loft, cricket is not a hobby or a pastime. It is his work, his profession, his means of survival. The sport that is a game to us is life for him in every sense of the word. And it's not just his life. We do not let it remain so. He is public property, deployed in the national interest. His life becomes a responsibility, a way to realize the dreams of a billion people, to uphold the pride of a nation. We claim his success, his fame, his records and achievements as ours.

But what of his failures? Whose are those? Where does

our claim to them stand? Do we give up on our dreams? Or do we find other ways to fulfil them?

There is no doubt that public memory is short. People's prayers for a fallen hero last only for a while. He becomes the object of occasional sympathy, and soon his name becomes a memory. Another player takes his place. The nation and the team move on. No one needs him anymore.

This is the fate that awaited one of India's stars of the 2011 World Cup, Yuvraj Singh, the bubbly, curly-haired boy from Chandigarh. There he was in March 2011, a phenomenon. Electric blue, in body and soul, he went on to annihilate anything that came in front of him. Three hundred and sixty-two (362) hard-earned runs, 15 precious wickets, four consecutive 'man of the match' awards. He didn't seem human. He was beyond mortal. The nation is spread over thousands of miles, but his fans and admirers were at every nook and corner. As he strode onto the pitch like a storm, a million lips chanted his name, wishing him luck, wishing him strength, wishing him victory. In those moments, he made us proud of being who we were, of being Indian, of being India.

We wished him all the luck in the world. But the luck didn't last long. He ran out of it.

How can prayers go so wrong? How could it happen to him? Did we fall short in our prayers? Did the million lips stop chanting or was their chant useless now that their lips were so puffed with pride?

When the 2011 World Cup came around, Yuvi was a crucial member of the Indian team. I have often wondered what the headlines in newspapers and on news channels would have screamed, had Yuvi pulled out because of a cough. Could he have told his captain that he couldn't play the next match because he had been coughing too much?

What would the Indian fan who had come to the stadium to see him bat say when he heard this? What would your reaction have been as you sat in front of the TV in your living room?

Years ago, when Dilip Vengsarkar dropped out of the Indian team in the semi-final against England in the 1987 World Cup because of a painful throat, they branded him a coward. Could Yuvi have risked that kind of criticism?

Schoolboys can complain of a cough when they want to bunk school. A man who had hit six sixes in an over could not do that. Not when he was in the middle of a World Cup. Yuvi could not, would not, say it out loud. Going back was not an option. Forget what people might say. Would he have been able to face himself if India had not won the Cup because of his absence? No. The aim was clear, the goal was set. For Yuvi, it was a matter of life and death. The World Cup had to be won.

As he went from match to match, the cough became more severe, disturbing his sleep and fitness schedule. He relied more on medication and the advice of his physio, whom he trusted implicitly. He started feeling breathless. He vomited every time he ate anything. Nothing they did helped his cough but he kept going, almost as if the cough pushed him to perform.

Ironically, the cough was getting louder and louder, but no one seemed to hear it. Nobody saw him in any sort of discomfort on the field. He batted sensibly, bowled with a plan and purpose and fielded with exceptional alertness. But the louder the cough became, the deeper it was getting into his system.

It was affecting his peace of mind, making him weak. But such is human psychology that when we are doing well, problems appear smaller. We remember all that we have done to reach this position and having got there, want to cherish the moment. Even the physical discomfort becomes bearable. Undoubtedly, success is the best medicine.

Yuvi did not take his cough seriously. He thought his body could bear the pain, as it had done on so many occasions. He overlooked the wear and tear that it had undergone over the years, the tremendous strain it had been subjected to. 'He was coughing and vomiting all

8

through the tournament. But we thought it was just the stress, and his desire to excel on the biggest stage, so we ignored it,' says his mother, Shabnam Singh.

And Yuvi kept burning, like the candle who gives light to the world by burning itself out.

The World Cup was just one more occasion when fate had challenged him. This time, too, he accepted the challenge. And by doing so, he chose the path of near self-destruction. With every match he played, his condition deteriorated further.

Eventually India won the World Cup. Yuvi was crowned the man of the tournament. And now he too forgot the sound of the cough amidst the applause and the adulation.

Then came the Indian Premier League (IPL), and with it began Yuvi's duties as the captain of the most expensive team in the tournament, the Pune Warriors of India. The extreme heat of summer and the non-stop travelling meant that Yuvi had no time for rest or recovery. The cough was back, and it occurred to him that something had to be done. But if the responsibility of representing the nation is great, isn't there a huge responsibility attached to being bought for such a whopping sum? How could he let down those who had placed so much trust in his abilities?

Yuvi had managed to ignore the cough during the World Cup because it hadn't affected his performance, but a week into the IPL, his body revolted. His World Cup form deserted him. Within a month, he was looking like a shadow of himself. The cough had settled in his body; he was struggling. But he was the captain of the team. He couldn't afford to sit out. He wanted his team to win and they weren't winning.

The season ended with a dismal performance by Yuvi's team, which must have left him a very unhappy man.

At every critical juncture of his career, Yuvi has been thwarted by fate. This time, however, in the last week of May, providence intervened in a positive way. He was invited to inaugurate a clinic in Delhi after IPL 2011 and he allowed himself to be examined. The doctor who examined him claimed that he noticed a patch in the lungs that looked dangerous.

'After all the excitement and the celebrations, we went for medical advice when the problem (of his cough) persisted,' says Yuvi's mother.

'To our horror, we found a golf-ball-sized lump over his left lung.' Yuvi had what in medical terms is called a lymphoma, an abnormal tumour.

The family was incredulous. 'We were devastated. We

10

just couldn't accept it. He had had bouts of coughing for a long time, but we had been told it was common allergy to dust and pollution.'

Yuvi himself was indignant. 'I didn't believe the reports,' he said. 'I felt fine, and deep inside, I felt good too,' he remembers, almost embarrassed to go into the painful details.

When the time came to pick the team for the West Indies tour of June–July 2011, Yuvi was thrilled to find himself in. It had been a long cherished dream to play in the Test team. At that point though, he decided to share a part of his agony. He dropped out of the tour, citing a lung infection. He was very weak and had been advised complete rest for a month, after which he was expected to be as good as new.

At that stage, Yuvi went into a shell. 'He became quieter and endured everything in the privacy of his home; he made sure nobody got to know about it,' his mother remembers. But he never gave up hope nor, indeed, did he give up on life. 'Initially, we couldn't take it; it was too painful even to look at Yuvi,' says Shabnam. 'It wasn't just the fear that is associated with the dreaded word that gnawed at us; it was unbearable to see the way he suffered. He was in excruciating pain all the time.'

Yuvi underwent rigorous treatment and, at the same

time, gingerly resumed practising his game. Early medical treatment and therapy made him feel better, and eager to resume his India duties. He was bent on getting fit and didn't want anything to come in the way of the England tour in July–August 2011. It was Test cricket calling again, the dream that he had been chasing ever since he started playing the game.

The dream made him drag himself forward. But once again, it was not to be. When he arrived in England, looking overweight and not in the best shape, he was almost an object of ridicule. Nobody knew the trauma he was going through or the fact that, for quite some time, he hadn't been able to do even the basic drills. Only his closest friends in the Indian team were aware of his condition. In the second Test, he scored a gritty 62 and finally vindicated his inclusion. Tragically, injury came between Yuvi and his Test dream once again. But this time, it did more good than harm. He broke his finger and had to return home. The phrase 'a blessing in disguise' was surely coined for this occasion. 'I needed rest. My body needed a break. That's when I realized the big truth: I can't fight time. I can't fight my own body,' Yuvi admitted, almost heartbroken.

The early return home gave Yuvi time to get a proper medical check-up. For three months or so, he went for one scan after another, one test after another, practically looking death in the eye every day. The reports indicated that the tumour was non-malignant and non-threatening and could be treated through medication and therapy. Through all this, Yuvi kept a smile on his face, and held onto the faith instilled in him by his Guruji. 'We were all worried. But he would only keep telling us one thing. I am a brave boy, I will come out of this, he would say,' his mother recalls.

Everyone was relieved beyond measure that the tumour was not malignant. Family and friends couldn't thank god enough.

'For the first time in a long while, I had a big smile on my face. My mom was jumping all around in joy. I was ready to take on life again,' said Yuvi. Only such experiences make you realize the value of life. In the words of Yuvi, 'Appreciate life. Enjoy all its small successes and sweet moments. I realized then that health is the most important thing. Money, fame, cars, adulation, these count for nothing.'

He was back on course towards rehabilitation. 'I do yoga in the morning and light training in the evening. In a week's time, I should be practising like normal. I will be ready for the one-dayers in Australia,' he declared in February that year. 'I just can't wait to have that India logo on my shirt again. I want to wear that India cap again. I can't wait to play cricket. That's what my life is all about.' His voice quivered with emotion.

'He couldn't return to full gym-work yet. He would get breathless in no time. But he would just not give up,' Shabnam says.

Then, just before the West Indies tour of India, Yuvi realized that there might be an opportunity to play the visitors. To prove his fitness, he insisted on playing a Twenty20 match for Punjab. The previous night, he had undergone some tests and his arm was swollen. He couldn't even move it properly. But he refused to listen. He didn't want to lose another opportunity.

Though he did get to be part of the Indian team, Yuvi's poor form continued and he scored only 23, 18 and 25 in the two Tests. And he wasn't called upon to bowl at all.

The selectors dropped him from the third Test of the series, choosing to give younger players a chance.

The message was clear: Yuvi was not going to Australia for the Test series. It must have been one of the saddest days of his life.

In the midst of all this, on 12 December 2011, Yuvi celebrated his thirtieth birthday. It was a quiet day spent with his family and close friends. 'It feels different, it's like a new life for me,' Yuvi said, a day after the muted celebrations. 'It's almost like I am starting over again.' He was unable to subdue the joy and excitement in his voice.

A new beginning seemed to await Yuvi. He wasn't the kind to mope or live in the past. 'The New Year is round the corner. I am hoping it will bring fresh tidings. People around me are happy. I am happy,' he said. He expected to be in the team for the ODIs against Australia.

Soon, the tough phase would be past for Yuvi. Or so it seemed.

What happened next took everyone by surprise. The tumour that had been dismissed as non-malignant was found to be malignant. What had seemed to be a harmless, short-lived ailment was given a deadly name: cancer.

The same fate that had placed obstacles in his career path this time played a benevolent role. Yuvi's cancer was detected in the first stage itself. And as he underwent chemotherapy in the United States, his physio reassured us that the cancer was fully curable and that Yuvi would be fit to play by May.

'I know I am a good person. I have only done good things in life. So I knew something so bad could not happen to me,' Yuvi had said earlier, at a time when the cancer hadn't been diagnosed. But cancer or not, this statement holds good. As Yuvi played the innings of his life against the most deadly opponent ever, one realized that a sportsman can't stop being a sportsman in other areas of his life. Sport is not a profession, it isn't a skill to be learnt and imitated. Sport is a way of life, a way to be. And once it's in your system, you can't take it out. It becomes part of you, it defines your approach to life and everything you do.

Yuvi decided not to fight his battle in isolation. He found inspiration in another sportsman who had escaped death – Lance Armstrong, who fought testicular cancer to make the Tour de France his own for seven years in a row. Posted Yuvi on Twitter, 'I look forward to meet Lance Armstrong soon and take inspiration! Till then good bye, will keep you updated about my health.'

Actively posting photographs and posts on social networking sites strengthened him further. 'Thank you again to all my friends back home! I'm recovering well ... yes, it's tough but tough times don't last, tough men do! I will fight and come back as a stronger man cause I have the prayers of my nation...' he wrote.

Yuvi played this game too in the true spirit of sports-manship.

Chapter Two

A PROPHECY NAMED YUVRAJ

Life has a habit of throwing challenges at us. Some of us succumb to them, others stand up and fight them so we don't fall. But fighting isn't learnt in boxing rings. A fighter is made out of circumstances. Yuvraj Singh is one such fighter. He was turned into one by his father. A father who had decided that his son had to be a world-class cricketer.

Yograj Singh, a contemporary of Kapil Dev, was a right-arm medium-pace bowler who had played first-class cricket. In 1979 he had been selected to play for the Board President's XI against Pakistan in Baroda. But before this match, Yog had played only two Ranji matches in two seasons. After the Baroda match, I got him into the Mafatlal team. The team comprised stalwarts like Ashok Mankad, who was the captain, Eknath Solkar, Brijesh Patel and Parthasarthy Sharma. Yograj swears by the impact Mumbai had on him as a cricketer. Within a year, he found himself on a plane with the Indian team, ready for the tour of Australia, New Zealand and Fiji in the 1980–81 season.

But the dream did not last. Yograj played just one Test and six ODIs and had very little success. He is the first to admit that he didn't do justice to his talent.

I remember that from 1979 till 1982, when he was with Mafatlal, he worked very hard at his game and the cricketing fraternity of Mumbai felt he deserved a second chance with the Indian team. But that was not to be. And as it turned out, Yograj's second chance would come to him, not directly but indirectly, through his son.

When Shabnam, Yog's petite and charming twenty-year-old wife, gave birth to a 3.8 kg baby boy, the entire family rejoiced but Yog was already making plans for the boy's future, unknown to the rest of them. By the time they returned home from PGI Hospital in Sector 12, Chandigarh, with the newborn, the father had it all worked out.

Yograj's first reaction to Yuvi's birth was, 'I will make him achieve what I could not.' From that moment, his son

18

was fated to live out his father's unfulfilled dreams and thwarted ambitions.

As the little boy grew up, he became very fond of skating. One day, he ran home excited after winning the sub-junior championship in school. His achievement was not appreciated. Yog threw away the skates and warned him never to take part in a skating competition again. Yuvi could only become a cricketer; his competitiveness had to be preserved for cricket.

With the Shivalik hills in the background of their Sector 11B house, Shabnam tended their beautiful garden where many colourful flowers bloomed. But what did the beauty of frail flowers mean to a man who wanted to make his son as strong as a rock! Yog first built a gymnasium on the first floor of their house, then he converted the lovely garden into a small pitch. He bought a dozen bats and tennis balls and he and Yuvi would practise from morning till night. Academics became secondary. As did everything else.

In the freezing Chandigarh winter, Yograj would drag Yuvi out of bed early in the morning so they could go to the ground. Once, when I was at their home, I heard Yuvi cry out around 10 p.m. I rushed out and saw the boy rubbing his chest. He had been hit by a wet tennis ball. The pink chest of the twelve-year-old had become black and blue. But all he could do was wait for the pain

19

to lessen and then get back to facing the wet tennis balls from seventeen yards away. I tried to convince Yog that twelve hours of practice would kill the child's enjoyment, but Yog had other ideas. His son must learn the game the hard way.

Bishan Singh Bedi has often said, 'Nobody should take any credit for chiselling Yuvi except his father, who really stuck into him during the early days in an absolutely ruthless manner, both physically and mentally.'

Even as a twelve-year-old, Yuvi was bigger and stronger than most boys his age. He once broke a sink simply by leaning on it. Says Angad Bedi, Bishan Singh Bedi's actor–son and a teammate of Yuvi's from the age of eleven, 'It was one of the first Bishan Bedi cricket camps held in Delhi. Yuvi was staying at the Jawaharlal Nehru stadium. The facilities were basic. There were no showers, hence only bucket baths were possible, and the loos had to be shared. One morning Yuvi got up to brush his teeth and as he leaned on the sink, it suddenly crashed to the ground. All hell broke loose then, and Yuvi's mum was called down from Chandigarh to sort the matter out with my dad. Clearly, Yuvi did not realize his own strength.' He adds, with a smile, 'My dad always had a big soft corner for Yuvi.

'He used to be a fab dancer and a mimicry artist. He loved dancing to the song "*Muqabla subhanallah laila*". He could pop, lock and do all the moves and everyone loved to

20

watch him dance. No gathering was ever complete in the camp without his dance performance. He was loved by all, he was so charming and innocent as he still is.'

The senior Bedi says, 'During his formative years, Yuvi was a bundle of energy and up to loads of mischief, often bordering on indiscipline. There were times when I'd drive him six or seven kilometres down the hill at Chail and then tell him to get off and jog behind my vehicle all the way up.

'Yuvi was unusually big for his age. He was hugely talented and hit the ball really hard. In our summer camps in Chail in Himachal Pradesh, while lads his age struggled to reach the ropes, Yuvi would clear them easily. We'd lose many balls thanks to his big shots. In fact, he enjoyed hitting the ball out of sight so it could not be retrieved from down the hill. We had to stop him by declaring him out if the ball went over the hill.

'I must admit I was in absolute awe when he hit six sixes in an over – both Sir Gary and Ravi Shastri had done a similar job against an ordinary spinner, but Yuvi took on a promising English seamer! I reckon Yuvi could've done it again considering the quality of modern bats and also the amount of cricket that is being played. But he does not play for records. He reminds me of Kent and England's left-hander Frank Woolley with his lazy elegance.'

Angad Bedi recollects how Yuvi was reluctant to go to the summer camp at Chail. 'My dad and I, specially went to his nana-nani's house in Panchkula, where he was hiding, to take him along. He just did not want to go. He was dragged out of the house by my ever-so-strict dad.

'Yuvi is a true friend. When he was a teenager he bought a Maruti Zen and the first thing he did was take me for a long drive. We chatted a lot and he seemed very happy. After playing for India, one day I got a call from him that he wanted to take me for a long drive. This time he came in an expensive BMW. I cherish these memories because on each occasion, he remembered me. That's called true friendship.'

Yuvi's six-hitting ability might have been noticed by the world only after he got six sixes in an over, but those who saw him play as a boy always knew he had it in him.

In 1997, when Yuvi was just sixteen, he was sent to Mumbai. This was the stage that Yograj had been preparing him for all these years. Yuvi didn't need any pushing now. His father had made sure that enduring hardships came easily to him.

Yuvi stayed with me at Andheri and practised at Dilip Vengsarkar's academy at Churchgate. He was a tough boy, but the fast pace of Mumbai life got to him sometimes. In Chandigarh, too, his life had been tough, but at least the serene surroundings gave him some comfort and peace. Once, as he stood on the crowded Andheri platform, he said to me, 'Mac uncle, Bombay is full of people. Chandigarh is full of trees.'

Getting into the crowded train at Andheri with his cricket kit to reach Churchgate at 8 a.m. was only a preliminary ordeal for him. At Vengsarkar's academy, he showed the Mumbai boys how one could practise from morning to evening even in the Mumbai heat. By the time he boarded the train at Churchgate at 6 p.m., he had no energy left. When he expressed his resentment at the hectic schedule, I reminded him, 'Yuvi, all those boys who practise with you also travel long distances. In fact, many of them travel from suburbs like Vasai, Virar, Thane and Kalyan.' He nodded his head. He understood.

Yuvi loved fielding and he was most impressive as a fielder, diving and stretching for the ball. He practised his pick up and return to either end of the pitch diligently. After a month, he accompanied the academy team to Satara, a town in Maharashtra. Ojas Mehta, the captain of the team, recalled those days for me.

'The Satara trip was one of the most memorable trips of our cricketing careers. All of us who were a part of the team still remember the time spent there, and often talk about it when we meet. A couple of times, when I met Yuvi, he had that wide and genuine smile of his as we went down memory lane. That was the first cricket tour for most of the team, including Yuvi. We were so exhilarated at the prospect of the tour that we were together all the time, from breakfast to the last goodnight. The other reason for that was that there was nothing to do in Satara. We were staying in Rajatadri hotel. Yuvi's room-mates were Aniruddha Dichwalkar, Sushant Manjrekar and Kapil Parpillewar.'

Not only did Yuvi have ample talent and a big heart, he also had a big appetite. Ojhas remembers having dinner at Gulmohur restaurant every day while they were in Satara. 'While two or three players shared a butter chicken between them, Yuvi used to have two kheema parathas all by himself. The cook was specially instructed by him to polish the parathas with extra butter!'

'Yuvi was such a team man that he never had a problem batting at any number. He was our number four batsman, but when I thought he could be utilized higher up the order, he agreed and batted at number three. In the last two games, he opened the innings as well. Fielding was always Yuvi's strong point. His favourite position was at backward point. But he was brilliant anywhere and at gully he took a couple of extraordinary catches, diving forward on that rough, uneven brown soil of the Satara ground which had not a single blade of grass on it. It was like diving on a tar road.

'Like every Punjabi, Yuvi too loved music. On the tour, while everyone else had Walkmans, Yuvi owned a discman. But his favourite music wasn't Punjabi. It was the Spice Girls,' recounts Mehta. 'I used to like it too and we used to listen to it at the same time, one earphone in my ear and the other in Yuvi's. Our favourite song was "*Mamma*".

'We all were pranksters at heart, and so was Yuvi. Together, we troubled people walking near the hotel. We used to scare them with laser pens. That trip is deeply engraved in all our hearts.'

In 1997 Yuvi toured England with the Star Cricket Club of Mumbai, managed by Kailash Gattani, the former Rajasthan player. Recounts Gattani, 'As a sixteen-year-old, he came with me on the tour of England in 1997 and was a huge success. He was a brilliant batsman and had guts. In one of the matches, we were stuck with the most difficult call that any Test team faces. We could either draw the game or risk it and go for the runs. To me and others in the team, a draw was the best and most practical option. But Yuvi had confidence. He wanted to win. He batted and we won the game with a few overs to spare. I remember that even with long on and long off up, he kept hitting huge sixes.'

Yuvi's penchant for the big shots was his hallmark even in those days. Remembers Balwinder Singh Sandhu, 'I first met Yuvi when I was conducting the Punjab Cricket Association camp in 1997. He was very talented, but loved to loft the ball. He was a bit confused because his coaches had told him not to do it. Perhaps they were right because he sometimes lofted without proper technique. As a result, he would be caught in the deep. I showed him the correct technique and I saw that he practised it sincerely.'

All along, Dilip Vengsarkar kept encouraging him to play with aggression. Dilip is a firm believer in batsmen playing their natural game. He was convinced that Yuvi would learn from his mistakes, which he did. Too much technical lingo could have confused him.

After returning from the England tour with Gattani's team, I noticed a huge change in Yuvi. He had scored the highest number of runs on the tour and tightened his game, but most importantly, he finally understood the values of the game.

With strict and rigorous training, the chocolate boy of Chandigarh became a strong north Indian man. He was no longer the victim of bullies, and even began to challenge the older boys with confidence. At the same time, he began to love the game. The harder he worked, the deeper the realization dug in that playing for India was not going to be as easy as he had thought it would be.

The Mumbai experience proved invaluable for Yuvi. Former Test player Vikram Rathore, under whom Yuvi played for Punjab, remarks, 'When Yuvi made his first-class debut at sixteen in 1997, he got out for zero. He was very upset. In fact, over the years, I found that contrary to his body language, which was casual, he was very serious about cricket. When he failed, it affected him. A year after practising at Vengsarkar's academy and going to England with Gattani's team, he came back as a mature cricketer. Amazingly fit and confident, he was fielding brilliantly and began to play some impact knocks.'

Yuvi first made it big when he captained the Under-19 Punjab cricket team in the final of the Cooch-Behar Trophy against Bihar Under-19s. He scored 358 at the Keenan Stadium in Jamshedpur.

Very soon, it became clear that tense situations got the best out of Yuvi. Punjab all-rounder Reetinder Singh Sodhi, a close friend of Yuvi's, describes an incident that took place during the semi-final of the U-19 World Cup against Australia in the year 2000. 'We were 3 down for 180 in the forty-fourth over. Yuvi was the next batsman and I was to go in after him. 180 in 44 overs was no score. We were all worried. Yuvi turned around and told me, "Don't worry, I'm there." He went in to bat in the forty-fifth over and hit a huge six. In the next twenty-five balls, he made 58 runs with 5 sixes and 5 fours.'

Yuvi's performance in that tournament became a talking point all over the country. India was looking for a big hitter down the order, and Yuvi was not only a big hitter but a brilliant fielder. At backward point, his swift movements, pick up and throw made it difficult for any batsman to steal a single. Shots which would have made it to the boundary were intercepted. Most importantly, his throw back to either side of the pitch was fast and tremendously accurate. India hadn't seen much fielding of this kind. It was a revolution.

Roger Binny, coach of the World Cup winning U-19 team, says that Yuvi first came to his notice at the nets in Sri Lanka, just before the tournament started. 'He was timing the ball so well and hitting all the bowlers so effortlessly that I didn't feel the need to tell him anything. Everything came naturally to him. His brilliance and form showed in the game against the Australians when he toyed with their attack which was actually very good. The coach of the Australian team, Rod Marsh, was really impressed.'

Those first few years in Mumbai proved to be really crucial for Yuvi. Hundreds come to Mumbai every day to fulfil their dreams. It was so then, and it is the same now. But Mumbai is not kind to everyone. Some fade away because of bad luck and lack of opportunity, some because they get carried away. Yuvi made the best of Mumbai. It taught him a great deal about life and he acknowledges it. It is only fitting then, that he has decided to make this city his home.

Yuvi always loved tennis and might have pursued it. He felt it did not put the same kind of pressure on him as playing cricket often did. His resentment against team sports grew stronger when he was dropped after his debut Ranji game against Orissa in 1997. For two years after that, he only played junior cricket.

Yuvi was deeply upset that his destiny could be shaped by the needs of a team. He believed that he could make his own destiny and control it. But he forgot that his destiny had been written the day he was born. He had to play cricket. He was made for it, if not by the gods, then by his father.

Cricket might not have been Yuvi's natural choice of sport, but he had become a natural cricketer for sure. Yograj Singh, his father, had demonstrated how one does not have to be born with any inherent inclination towards a sport. Traits can be developed. Interest can be inculcated. With the right amount of perseverance, nature can be overcome.

Chapter Three

TESTING TIMES

We often think of life in terms of black and white: positive or negative, good or bad, success or failure. But a lot exists between these binaries. Is killing in self-defence a positive or a negative act? Is giving money to a beggar good or bad? And how do we assess or define success? Is the chaiwala who starved for days to send his daughter to school successful or not? Should the smartest scientist in the world be called successful if his children despise him?

It is not easy to justify labelling someone a success or a failure. An individual may excel in some areas while being utterly incompetent in others. Should he be called a success for his skill or a failure for the lack of it?

This question is most pertinent in the case of Yuvraj Singh. Mention his name on the streets and people will tell you about his six sixes and breathtaking dives. Say the name in the commentary box and the pundits will stroke their chins and ponder.

Talented though he is, Yuvi's abilities have always been a point of discussion when the experts within the cricketing fraternity try to understand him. It is difficult to explain why someone who has been a part of the Indian dressing room for more than a decade has not been able to make a mark in Test matches and cement his place in the Test squad. Yet his performance in the shorter version of the game is right up there with the best. Rahul Dravid, who had quite a few partnerships with Yuvi, says, 'No doubt Yuvi is immensely talented and one of the best players in one-dayers. In fact, he is in my list of the World's best XI. But he certainly hasn't lived up to his potential in Test matches. I have seen him getting a hundred against the likes of Shoaib Akhtar, Umar Gul and Mohammad Asif, but by and large, the impact that he has had in one-dayers, he hasn't had in Test matches.'

It is tempting to say that fate has played a large part in shaping Yuvi's Test career. If one looks at it rationally, it is clear that selection to a team depends on three factors. The primary one, of course, is the player's own performance. Then comes the form of the other players, injuries to potential team members and the player's own physical fitness. Every player, at some level or the other, has to negotiate these three factors. But there are some others which are, in a sense, beyond his control.

The game of cricket by its very nature depends a great deal on extraneous factors: the wind, the rain, the moisture, the pitch, the grass, the toss, the crowd, the edge, the nick, the no-ball, the fumble, the skid, the crack, the dew, the sunlight, the floodlights – any one factor goes against you, and a won match is lost. When a player is in good form, he can overcome all these obstacles.

Similarly, one day you could bowl well without getting any wickets while someone who is bowling rubbish at the other end gets a fiver. When you are middling the ball perfectly and feeling confident, all of a sudden you get a snick and you are gone. Another time, you might be struggling, missing the line, edging the ball in different directions, but catches get spilled and you end up scoring a hundred, raising the bat to the pavilion and wondering how you got there.

Yuvi has met this god called Fate far too often in his Test career. It was as if someone was playing a game with him. For just when he thought that his greatest dream, of being a regular Test player, was going to be achieved, it would be snatched from his grasp. The innumerable occasions when he fell ill or got injured just when he was on the verge of securing his place in the Test team are a testimony to this. Either that, or he was out because the middle order was settled and performing well.

Even Yuvi's Test debut came to be almost by default. He got his Test cap in 2003 when India was playing New Zealand at Mohali, his home ground. Captain Sourav Ganguly was injured and Yuvi was chosen to take his place. Ganguly returned and Yuvi was dropped. He got another opportunity in the 2004 tour of Pakistan, again because of an injury to Ganguly. Yuvi knew he had to make the most of this opportunity. In the second Test at Lahore, he scored a century but India lost the match. When Ganguly returned for the third Test, it seemed that the selectors wanted to give Yuvi a regular place, for they dropped Aakash Chopra instead.

A player of Yuvi's calibre needed a mentor, and in Sourav Ganguly he found one. Yuvi worshipped him. Even in private conversations with me, his words have always reflected the tremendous respect he has for Dada. Dada tried to make him an opener like Sehwag, but somehow that move failed. After two poor performances in the Border–Gavaskar Trophy against Australia, he was dropped in favour of Gautam Gambhir.

It was 2005, and Sachin Tendulkar was suffering from a tennis elbow. Yuvi was sent for, and he batted at number six. Enter Greg Chappell, and Ganguly was sacked. This meant that Yuvi finally had a free spot. Ironically, it was his beloved captain's downfall that presented him with the opportunity he craved.

Yuvi scored a second Test century in the third Test in Pakistan in 2006, which India again lost. He struggled a bit after this and later in the year, he suffered a knee injury. This allowed Ganguly to return, and he went on to top-score in the series and seal his place in the team. In fact, Ganguly staged a comeback in the Test matches against South Africa in 2006: in 3 Tests he scored 214 runs with an average of 42.80.

One can only wonder at this duo, close friends tied together in a strange web. The downfall of one meant the rise of the other.

In 2007, in the third Test against Pakistan, Yuvi was again picked to replace an injured Sachin Tendulkar. India were 61/4 before Yuvi and Ganguly put on a 300-run partnership. Yuvi recorded his highest Test score of 169. But he had a very poor run again against Australia later that year and was dropped.

In view of all this, it was only natural for Yuvi to feel disgruntled. He could not secure a place in the final XI of the Indian team because of an abundance of experience and talent in the middle order.

You could say, of course, that he was lucky to get a look in whenever someone was injured. Many don't get to play even a single Test match. But only Yuvi knows the depth of frustration he experienced at the way things worked – and didn't work – for him.

Dilip Vengsarkar, who was the chairman of the national selection committee, says, 'Any type of injury puts a player back, especially when you are missing Test matches because of it. Yuvi had a knee injury playing kho-kho, a sport that is supposed to be played barefoot. He was playing with shoes on, and he paid a heavy penalty for it. When there is competition in the team, one has to be careful. It's not always the player's fault, but once he has had a knee or back injury, it makes him self-conscious in the field. He is not the same player after such injuries.'

That is exactly what happened to Yuvi. He got back after two and a half months of treatment, but when he returned, his swift movements had deserted him. Shrewd cricketer that he was, he made amends by using his experience in batting, and stopped risk-diving in the field. From playing swashbuckling knocks, he began to play percentage shots. In the T20s, though, he still used the sweet spots on the bat to perfection.

A school of coaches has pointed out flaws in Yuvi's technique. But it is equally true that when a stroke player is in the right mood, technique becomes subservient to talent. Once the ball starts connecting with the sweet spot of the bat and he gets the timing right, the boundaries start to come every now and again. What matters in the case of a stroke player like Yuvi is that he should play his natural game.

Vengsarkar, who has been observing Yuvi from his early days, says, 'I watched him get a century at Lahore and some of the Pakistan old-timers who had played against Gary Sobers compared him to Sobers. A very huge compliment.'

If you compare the footage, Yuvi matches Sobers shot for shot. Power combined with timing, the loft right out of the ground or the flick bisecting the field and racing to the boundary, Yuvi gives spectators something to cheer about. And they expect him to score at a brisk pace all the time. But even stroke makers like Sobers or Viv Richards, who had all the shots in the world, struggled at times.

The difference between those two and Yuvi is that they didn't play as many one-dayers as Yuvi has. Though the basics remain the same, a batsman has to change his approach and also his mindset. It requires a lot of adjustments for a stroke player. Perhaps Yuvi found it difficult. Perhaps, when the situation became the master and the player had to shift gears, he was not up to making the change. Besides, Yuvi had not even played Tests consistently, being in and out of the team, sometimes unjustifiably so.

The Sri Lanka tour of 2010 started well for Yuvi. He scored a superb 118 in a three-day game against Board President's XI. He clobbered the bowlers with 6 sixes and 11 fours. In the first Test, he scored 62 when India was struggling. He was preparing for the second Test when he fell ill with dengue. And Suresh Raina got a chance to make his Test debut. Raina scored a hundred. Yuvi was declared fit for the third Test, but he wasn't selected. That was a big setback for him.

Raina may have scored a hundred but Yuvi was fit and in form and he should have been brought back into the team. That day it dawned on Yuvi that he could never again take anything for granted. His self-belief was shaken. Too much had happened to him over the years. And how long could a person keep his self-belief intact when it looked like the gods were plotting against him?

Here was a player in smashing good form, right from the day he set foot in Sri Lanka, massacring the bowling at will and playing brilliantly even when the rest of the team was struggling, and yet he lost his place despite being fully fit. Any cricketer would want to know the logic behind such an exclusion, and even with the understanding that it is a team sport, no one would like to be treated so shabbily. Yuvi was reportedly not even informed of his exclusion beforehand. But then, we all know that such things happen in Indian cricket.

As those travelling with the Indian team have observed, these days it boils down to the captain-player relationship, and which player enjoys the captain's confidence. The decision-making and body language of Dhoni always indicated that though he would love to have Yuvi in the team, for some reason he preferred Raina.

The list of instances and explanations goes on, and Yuvi's Test career remains an enigma. 'It's like the gods are saying, No, Yuvraj, you can't play Test matches,' says his mother.

Are we banking too much on fate in the story of Yuvraj Singh? Can fate indeed be so vindictive? Can a fighter like Yuvi be swept away so easily, carried away on the waves like a sea shell?

How does a cricketer go from strength to strength in one format while being no good in another format of the same game? Are the formats more different than we assume them to be? Do we forget that cricket is not all about the bowler bowling and the batsmen hitting the ball? That the mind is the most vital driving force in the game, and different formats mean a different mindset, different in application, different in attitude?

Perhaps it wasn't about fate, opportunities or unfair decisions. Maybe the problem lay within Yuvi – not his talent, because that has never been in doubt. What has always been interesting is the way Yuvi deals with his talent, and his attitude.

Was there a mental game being played between Yuvi the cricketer and Yuvi the person?

Aunshuman Gaekwad was the coach of the Indian team when Yuvi first played for India in the ICC Championship in Nairobi. 'When I saw Yuvi first, he impressed me with his talent. He was eighteen then. In my strategy, I was looking for a left-hand batsman who could come in at number six and attack when it mattered in the fifty-over game. He was not only a very good batsman, but also a brilliant fielder. I told him to bowl more in the nets, which he did. He was very serious about the game, especially while fielding practice. Even though he was a junior, he would push seniors to go for the ball or a catch. The Nairobi grounds aren't big. I needed a batsman to clear infield and a fielder to stop boundaries. Yuvi did that admirably. I remember he scored 84 against the likes of McGrath and Brett Lee and hit them out of the field. That day a top star was born for Indian cricket.

'Once, during the tournament, he rushed to the dressing room and was in terrible pain as he just couldn't urinate. We tried everything, but nothing worked. Eventually, a local doctor treated him and the next moment he was on the ground. This was the level of his commitment.'

Perhaps Yuvi's flamboyant, go-getter attitude, which is often considered the main reason for his success in ODIs, is the biggest reason for his failure in Tests.

Balwinder Singh Sandhu remembers Yuvi the sixteen-year-old boy who, when corrected, practised the lofted shot diligently. But six years later, he found Yuvi a changed man. 'When I met him at the NCA in 2003,' says Sandhu, 'his ego was big. The NCA pitch had moisture and yet he kept playing and missing his off drive. I told him that on such pitches, he must not reach for the ball and must let the ball come to him. To defy me, he kept trying the same thing. Eventually, I told the fast bowlers to hit him in the ribcage so that he would go on the backfoot. He was hit by Harvinder Singh.'

Sandhu believes that Yuvi should have tightened his defence when he was young. 'He didn't, and he was exposed in the longer format of the game. He says that the difference between Viv Richards and Yuvi is that Viv wasn't arrogant when it came to the game. Viv played to his strengths. Yuvi didn't bother about the finer technicalities when the going was good.

'Yuvi's conviction and confidence that had taken him so far were starting to look like arrogance to many. He also seemed unnecessarily adamant.'

At the same time, younger players like Rohit Sharma speak about how compassionate Yuvi can be. Says Sharma, 'Yuvi really loves me. When the team for the 2011 World Cup was announced, I wasn't in the team. Naturally, I was disappointed. The moment he came to know, he came to my room and told me to get ready. He took me out for dinner and like an elder brother told me, "Look, such things will keep happening in cricket, but never show disappointment. If you have a dream of playing for India for a long time, then learn to fight. You have terrific talent and you will succeed. When it happened to me in the 2003 World Cup, it was Sachin who consoled me. Now I am telling you what Sachin told me."

'When he was dropped against West Indies and I replaced him, I was the first one to call him and I repeated what he had told me, but he sounded very disappointed. I must say he is a genuine friend.'

Says Kiran More, 'Yuvi is such a player that I will go miles to watch him bat. Amazingly talented, had he stayed focussed and concentrated on his game, he would have been more successful in Tests.'

More was the Chairman of the selection committee in

2004, and he remembers Yuvi telling him that he wanted to open the innings against Australia at Chennai in the second Test. He had batted in the middle order in the first Test at Bangalore. Says More, 'I told him that since he hadn't even opened for his state, he would be under pressure facing the very good attack of Australia, but apparently someone in the team had persuaded him to do it. My job was to advise him, but he wasn't convinced. He opened, and failed miserably. He talked to me later and admitted that he wanted to open simply because he wasn't getting a chance. It was a hard lesson he learnt.'

Yuvi's inability to come good in Tests did not remain a personal problem. It had become a point to ponder for all the critics of the game. Many greats tried to help him. A few, like More and Sandhu, seem to have taught Yuvi a lesson or two about the fundamental issues that he appeared to have with his batting and attitude. Somehow all this guidance did not have an effect on him, and he made the same errors again and again. He did learn, but the learning was short-lived and the old Yuvi always outgrew and overshadowed the new learning.

This had been his failing right from the start. Vikram Rathore, former Indian opener and Punjab captain, remembers an incident that took place in March 2002 at Faridabad. 'I think he had been dropped from the Indian team and had come down to Faridabad to play the Duleep

Trophy against South Zone. The pitch was slow and low and he came to bat at number three. I was at the other end. Left-arm spinner Sriram was bowling. They had a silly point and forward short leg. After every over, Yuvi said to me, "Paaji, I will clear the long on". I kept telling him not to be stupid. This went on for some overs. When he kept telling me the same thing, I asked him, "Yuvi, how many innings have you played this year?" He replied, "Around twenty." Then I asked him how many times he had got out in the deep and how many times at close in. He said he had got out many times in the deep but rarely when he was defending. I told him that he had answered my question. He realized the truth of the situation then, rethought his attitude, and scored a double hundred in that match.'

There are some things we will never figure out. What exactly went wrong with Yuvi? Why is it that one of our most talented cricketers could not establish himself in the Test team?

For Yuvi, too, it was a mystery and it left him feeling unhappy and frustrated.

But some good came out of all this. The constant waiting made Yuvi mentally stronger. Motivational autobiographies became staple reading for him, and they had the desired effect. His utterances became more reasoned. He began to articulate his point of view patiently, without any trace of impatience.

It didn't take long, though, for his volatile self to surface, especially when he sensed that he might miss out on captaincy. And especially because it was Vengsarkar, the chairman of the selection committee, who chose Mahendra Singh Dhoni over him.

Whatever the reasons for this, Yuvi realized that being in the Test team was a distant dream, but now even his place in the ODI team could come under threat in the upcoming 2011 World Cup.

He changed his approach to the game and began bowling more in the nets, something he had not done earlier. It was clear that he wanted to impress upon the team that he was capable of not only bowling economically but being effective in the middle overs.

Yuvi's marked improvement as a bowler gave the team management the luxury of having a genuine all-rounder. His value as a great finisher was always known, but when his pie chucker deliveries began to fox batsmen, there was no way he could be dropped. And it was when Yuvi realized that the going was good that he got into the frame of mind to make it even better.

Before the 2011 World Cup, Yuvi wasn't sure of getting

all the games but he worked hard on his bowling, became a percentage cricketer and more importantly, played to what the situation demanded. His preparation for the biggest stage of all had started in earnest.

Chapter Four

SHABNAM SINGH

A MOTHER SPEAKS

Shabnam Singh, Yuvi's mother, has seen a lot in life. She gave birth to a son who could not be hers. From the moment of his birth, her husband decided his fate. For Shabnam, every hour that her husband spent making Yuvi a cricketer was an hour lost with her son. In her husband's pursuit of his dream, her child was lost to her. Although she grieved, she could do nothing but watch him undergo the rigorous training his father put him through every day. She prayed and hoped that the day would come soon when her son reached the pinnacle that he was being trained for, so that the regimen could end.

It did, and Yuvi became a cricketer of the highest order. But perhaps it is in the nature of life to never let people be. Yuvi's career fluctuated dramatically. He earned a name for himself as a world-class one-day player, but he was not content with that. Both he and his parents believed that to be a great cricketer one had to make a mark as a Test player. And that was one thing that continued to elude him. But through it all, his mother stood by him. She celebrated his success, felt his pain, shared his disappointment.

Yuvi's decade-long career as a member of the Indian cricket team was not devoid of distress. Injury and form were two strange friends he had. The first presented itself at unexpected moments, and the second disappeared suddenly, without warning. The year before the World Cup was one of the worst for Yuvi as a cricketer, dogged as he was by injuries.

Says Shabnam, 'It was just one injury after another. Even on his birthday in 2010 he broke a finger; he had three injuries on the hand in one year. All the time, he was struggling with injuries. What happens is that you become defensive, and then people started saying, "Oh, he is not standing [fielding] there, he is not standing here." What do you expect? Obviously it affects your psychology. You feel that you are going to get injured again. But he fielded in his normal position in the World Cup. In Sri Lanka he was doing so well, getting a hundred in the practice match and a half-century in the next match. He couldn't play the one after that because he got dengue. Raina played and made a hundred and in the next match, Yuvi had to sit out. I think he went through a really miserable time then. Everyone tells him he is so talented, and then he feels frustrated that he can't cement his place in the Test side. He has just been very unlucky and something or the other always goes wrong when he is playing a Test match. In ODIs, everything falls into place. But during Tests, it's like God says, No, you can't be playing Test matches now. That's what we feel. So he has to accept it, and when the opportunity comes, he should take it.'

Shabnam's heart obviously aches when she hears unfair criticism of her son. 'Yes, he could never cement his place as a Test player. But that doesn't mean that he was taking things lightly. One thing Yuvi really hates is being a loser. Whether it is table tennis, cricket, hockey or snooker, if you defeat him, he'll practise ten times harder in a day and make sure that he comes back. That is the kind of fighting spirit he has. Being dropped from the side becomes a motivation for him. He works harder, reads books. He tells himself, I'm good and I will come back, and that is how he pushes himself. He was always focussed on cricket. Yes, of course it hurts a child when his parents are separated, but his focus never wavered because he knew he had to play.'

One thing Yuvi has never shirked is sheer hard work, says his mother. She recalls the time when he hurt himself while playing kho-kho. 'I remember it was 28 October. He went for an acupuncture session and 40-50 needles pierced his fingers each time. The doctor said he would cure him but he had to go to him for 20-25 days. Yuvi said he couldn't take so much pain, but he did. It was the most horrifying experience, but he went through it and came back to play after two and a half months.'

Once, while on tour, Yuvi suffered a ligament tear in the knee, and the doctor told him to exercise in water. He couldn't find a heated or covered pool so he went to an open-air pool in the December cold. Perhaps this capacity to endure pain was the result of the rigorous training he had at the hands of his father all through his childhood. 'I didn't want to toughen him up that much. It was his father,' Shabnam says. 'On his Ranji debut, Yuvi was out for a duck and his world shattered. The next time he went to play a game, he got jaundice and was dropped. Then they didn't want him to play as he was too young to play the Ranji trophy. So he never got a proper game till he played the U-19 and got the man of the series in the U-19 World Cup. That is how he got a place in the Indian team.'

The media and the public have been very harsh on her son, says Shabnam. 'Even when he was working hard for a comeback, the media portrayed what they wanted to portray. If he was just sitting and talking to a girl for a second, that picture would be all over and people would think, Oh, he's only talking to girls. They didn't see the hours of hard work he put in; the minute of relaxation was all they mentioned. It is Yuvi's passion to play for the country, and he puts in the same effort whether he is in the team or out of it. I remember, after losing the 2007 World Cup, Yuvi, Harbhajan and I had to take a flight to Delhi. We overheard two boys at the airport remarking, "Put Yuvi and Harbhajan together. Let's lock them in a room and don't let them go out." I remember Bhajji was very upset. I said to him, How does it matter? Now, after the World Cup victory, when Yuvi walks anywhere, people start clapping. This is not fair to cricketers.'

It is true that we fans are fickle. It's almost as if our support for cricket comes with a precondition, the assumption that since we support them, we have an equal right to assault them if they don't perform. This kind of support is not love but a mere barter. 'I scream for you, you'd better hit a six.' What is a cricketer supposed to feel about this? Can he ever feel any affection for such devotees who are prepared to kill their god if their prayers aren't answered?

'It doesn't get to him any longer,' says Shabnam. 'With

time, he has become more mature. But everybody likes being praised and nobody likes being insulted in public. Playing for the country is a matter of pride. You give your blood, sweat and tears on the ground. It takes a stupid person a single second to make a comment. They don't realize what they are saying. Anyway, cricketers have to take it in their stride.'

Shabnam remembers the stress on the players during the 2011 World Cup. 'The atmosphere was so stressful, so heavy. The players were just not talking to anybody. You couldn't talk about a sneeze at that time. If you were not well, it wasn't taken into consideration. It was all about winning.'

That's why Yuvi's persistent cough and vomiting passed off as a minor problem. He couldn't possibly have made a fuss about it.

Until it became impossible to deny the truth. Of cancer.

Shabnam recalls the horror of the early days. 'It was 23 May 2011 and we had gone for a regular check-up. The X-ray showed a black thing sitting over Yuvi's lungs. A piece of flesh that swelled up when he ran and affected his lung power and his breathing.'

'It was as if life stopped for a moment. Yuvi had been ill throughout the World Cup. He was coughing, vomiting,

51

and suffering from sleeplessness and a bad throat. But everyone thought it was because of the stress. I did too. Even during the IPL, we had consulted a doctor. He gave Yuvi some antibiotics and told him it was just a sore throat.'

On 25 May, the team of doctors in Delhi who had examined Yuvi called Shabnam and said they suspected he had a tumour in his lung. They added that they had done a Fine Needle test and the results weren't conclusive. Only further tests could confirm it. The word 'tumour' was enough to splinter Shabnam's world but there was a still a chink of hope. She wouldn't give in to despair, though all she could do was wait. 'It was very difficult for Yuvi. He was undergoing treatment and he started feeling better, but he didn't want to face it. He wanted to go on playing and just forget everything. He had faith that he would be fine after the treatment, so he stuck to it. It started showing results and then he started to play.'

Yuvi refused to believe that there was anything wrong with him. But whether this was pure optimism or he was in denial is a matter of conjecture. He continued to play and even went to England on a tour. But the finger injury forced him to come back home prematurely.

At this point, he decided to go in for further treatment. 'We went for further tests in October, and the first biopsy showed that the tumour was malignant.'

'When we got to know that the tumour was malignant, Yuvi said to me, "Don't worry, I'm going to come out of it." I was totally stunned, speechless. The only thing that ran through my head was that this couldn't be happening to me. I used to sit with him during his treatment, but sometimes I used to go away because it was very painful.'

Shabnam isn't the kind to break down easily. She was once a state basketball player and had handled tough situations on the court. Now she quietly handled the crisis off it. She knew that pressing the panic button would only magnify the problem.

'Even during this time of stress there was great self-belief, though people used to say all sorts of things. I can say that as a mother, it was at the back of my mind that this couldn't happen to my son. Of course it used to bother me a lot, but I never let it take over my life. Never thought something was really wrong with him till the final test results came. He was recovering well, he was fine, and he kept his morale up. So we just let time pass by till the second report came.'

Yuvi remained strong through this period and made sure that the illness interfered with his life as little as possible. When he went to England, he didn't talk about his illness. Not only did he hide the possibility of cancer from the rest of the world, he hid it from himself too. 'He kept saying that he was feeling good. He only told me that he had difficulty while breathing. It affected him, but it wasn't so much at that time. Somehow, he managed. He never complained to me,' says Shabnam.

Yuvi stayed focussed on the game. Even when the doctors told him to relax, he didn't want to do so. Shabnam remembers that he kept saying, '"When can I get on the field, when can I start playing?" But once he realized how serious the illness was, he understood that he needed to get fully fit and then come back. Half-measures weren't possible.'

No one knew Yuvi had been diagnosed with a rare germ cell cancer till Shabnam decided to make it public many months later, towards the end of 2011. People were shocked at the news, and especially at the fact that it had been hidden for so long and Yuvi had been playing international cricket all this while. There was just one reason behind not telling anyone about it earlier. 'Yuvi himself didn't believe that he was not well,' Shabnam says.

So the cricketer who was always in the spotlight and whom the media and critics alike had termed flamboyant and easygoing, had been suffering all this while, and silently. It is ironic that we see only the part of the star that shines. The more complex part remains on the other side, hidden in darkness.

Being diagnosed with a disease as deadly as cancer would come as a shock to anyone at any point in life. In Yuvi's case, it got to him when his career had finally reached its pinnacle at the World Cup, when it seemed as though things could only get better. No one knows the pain of this better than Shabnam.

It is said that the mother feels the pain every time a child is hurt. One can imagine how much pain this mother has gone through as her superstar son was overnight turned into a patient fighting for his life. Only Yuvi and those close to him know how difficult it was, with the word 'cancer' hovering over every conscious moment.

Even when the cancer was confirmed and his treatment began, Yuvi remained calm and firm. He was active on social networking sites so as to not lose touch with the world. He gained strength and inspiration from his well-wishers. Yuvi might have absorbed the pain, but it was visible on the mother's face. The days of chemotherapy were the most traumatic. She felt dizzy just looking at the number of needles that were thrust into her son's body. But Yuvi would calmly tell her to relax. He would assure her that he was fine. At other times he would just keep quiet, not uttering a word; sometimes he joked and smiled.

Shabnam recalls how difficult it was to get Yuvi into a taxi and to the hospital. Since they stayed in a hotel during the first stage of chemotherapy, she couldn't cook for him. But for the second chemo, they moved into an apartment.

Shabnam would be busy all day trying to make him feel better. She woke him up, fed him and cleaned his bed and room. Though Yuvi could hardly swallow anything, she kept trying to cook different dishes for him. He would throw up whatever he ate. He was like a child again. He would make a fuss about taking his medicines. He was cranky. He would not let Shabnam stay away from him for too long. Afraid of the world, he looked to her for comfort and stability. Like any child, he expected his mother to ease his pain. He tried to hide his suffering from her, but when he couldn't control it, he cried in her lap. He might have been crafted in the sternest manner possible, but that hadn't killed the child in him. He still needed his mother's warm embrace and reassurance.

It must be said here that from a very young age, the distance between his parents, their troubled marriage and subsequent separation had added to Yuvi's anxieties. Yograj Singh thinks that the problem with his son has been his lax attitude, his uncontrolled behaviour and his unrestricted social life. But Shabnam thinks that her son does enough of what he is supposed to do. 'I had never felt that there was a time or need to control him. He is a good boy, and he has been listening to us. Fortunately we have our Guruji in Punjab, and Yuvi listens to whatever he says. We have a very good guiding force, and we are grateful to God for it. Even during his illness, all the guidance was from Guruji. I don't guide him, it is Guruji who does it. So I never felt the need to control him.'

Shabnam never doubted her son's courage or his determination to overcome his illness. Nor does she doubt his ability to make a comeback. She believes that he has been an ideal son and a devoted cricketer. 'He can go to any extreme if you need him to. He is a tough boy. He is very determined,' she says.

Shabnam must have died a hundred deaths during Yuvi's illness and treatment. But she is a loving mother, and incredibly brave. Instead of fussing over Yuvi's condition and causing him more distress, she decided to be his strength. She became the rock on which Yuvi could rest and rise.

Chapter Five

YOGRAJ SINGH
THE FATHER'S STORY

Are great men born great or are they made great? This question is relevant to the story of a father who saw in his son a born player. But for Yograj Singh, that was not enough. His son had to be the greatest cricketer ever to have walked the earth.

The story of Yograj is a strange one. It is a tale of the desperation of a man whose every breath was filled with the guilt of not having been successful in his preferred career. It is the tale of a man's vision, and his obsession with this vision, which made him blind to everything else in life.

All Yograj knew was that his son was to fulfil the promise that he himself had belied. The son had to lessen the burden of his father's past, and lay the ghost that refused to leave him.

Unfair though it may be to make your child bear the baggage of your own past, one thing is clear. Yograj succeeded in making Yuvi what he is.

Yograj Singh's cricketing career had started off well. He was a contemporary of Kapil Dev. Both men were from Chandigarh and both were very good all-rounders. In fact, former India captain Col. Hemu Adhikari rated Yograj a notch higher than Kapil Dev. For the India U-22 team that played against England in 1977 at Nagpur, Yograj was chosen over Kapil Dev.

But after 1977, for some reason, Yograj lost his way and was out of cricket for a couple of years. When I watched him at the nets at DAV College, Jullundur, in 1979, he still looked a very good all-rounder, though he weighed not less than 95 kg.

In those days, I was writing for *Sportsweek* magazine. I happened to be in Jullundur for some work and had requested Ashwini Minna, the former Punjab Ranji player who had played with Kapil Dev and Yograj Singh, to invite young talent to nets at DAV College. As the nets were going on, Yog arrived, and without looking at anyone, bowled and batted superbly. Though he looked overweight, in terms of skill, he was terrific. On my return to Mumbai, I mentioned to Polly Umrigar, the chairman of the selection committee, that I saw great potential in Yograj Singh. On the committee were experienced cricketers like Ghulam Ahmed, Chandu Sarwate, Dattu Phadkar and Vijay Mehra. They were aware that Yograj hadn't played much competitive cricket – in two seasons, he had played only two Ranji games – yet they picked him for the Board President's XI to play the touring Pakistan team at Baroda in 1979.

In that match, Yograj took 3 for 29, including the wickets of Javed Miandad and Wasim Raja off consecutive balls. Subsequently, he was picked for the Indian team that toured Australia and New Zealand in 1981. But he failed to perform, and from that point on, he simply faded away.

It is against this backdrop that Yograj's behaviour towards his son needs to be considered. In his mission to make Yuvi the greatest cricketer, the end became all important, the means didn't matter.

People called him a madman. And a madman he was. How many people are capable of such passion, such determination, perseverance, desire? The world laughed at Yograj, but he didn't care about their criticism. All he wanted was a son. Once he had him, he took charge. Luck and chance didn't matter because he would call the shots. He made the choices, he took the decisions. He constructed Yuvi bit by bit.

But his creation turned against him.

What follows is Yograj Singh Bundhel's version of his life and his relationship with his son, in his own words.

'I owe a lot to Mumbai, to you, Makarand, for resurrecting me and recommending my name to the national selectors. I always felt that I had left something incomplete. That caused me a lot of sorrow because you gave me so many opportunities, you got me a job with Mafatlal, which had the best team in India, you made me play cricket in Mumbai. Mafatlal taught me the cricket culture.

'Whatever I achieved, how to be a mature cricketer, I learnt in Mumbai. Yet I lived with this constant pain, this awareness, this feeling, that my life was somewhat incomplete, and I felt answerable to you, Makarand, to my parents, and to myself. Despite possessing so much talent and playing on such a big platform, I couldn't achieve much, partly because my family imposed certain restrictions.

'Sometimes I wish I had not thought about my parents. I wish I had not thought about my family. I should have focussed on my cricket and I would have been the greatest cricketer on earth. But I had to, because of a few reasons.

'So it was always in my heart that my family should have at least one cricketer in it. My attention went towards Yuvi because sport was in his blood. He was good at everything, from tennis to skating. I believed that he was a very talented sportsman, blessed by the gods. I felt like making him a cricketer because if you are a good athlete who has outstanding talent, you will be successful wherever you invest that talent.

'So I forced him. One day, when Yuvi came home after winning a skating competition, my first thought was that my son was doing such a fantastic job in this sport, winning so many medals. But when I looked at him, his red band and long mane, something hit me very hard. I threw away his skates and his medals. People called me a ruthless man, but I had something else in my mind. Yuvi was twelve years old at that time.

'I remembered people like Ashok Mankad and Sunil Gavaskar, under whom I played, telling me that all the important qualities should be inculcated from childhood itself. I remembered you telling me that one can do only one thing properly in life, not ten. So start whatever you are going to do at the earliest.

'I still feel that if I wanted to do something for a child, I'd do it when he was seven or ten. There are many players in my academy whom I spotted when they were eight or nine years old. And so I forced Yuvi to give up skating, which he loved. Obviously, he cried a lot that day. He would never cry in front of me, but that day he did. Even today, I don't like people crying.

'My wife and I had an argument that day because she didn't like what I had done. But I said, "This is not the job of women. Just shut up."

'My mother was also very angry and scolded me. But once Yuvi was tired of crying, I hugged him and told him that there was no future in skating. I tried to make him understand. I don't know if he remembers, but I explained to him that one thing still remains incomplete in me and I feel answerable to those who invested so much time in me, for time is nothing but money.

'That day, for the first time, a father cried in the arms of his twelve-year-old son. He hugged me like a mature person. Maybe he realized then, that from now on he would have to play cricket.

'Tea used to be served in my room every morning – Shabnam used to bring it in. The day after the skating incident, I remember he came in with her and asked me, "Will you come with me to buy a cricket kit or should I go

63

with Mom?" I was very happy. They went and bought the kit and Yuvi started playing.

'The first thing I did was take over the garden that Shabnam had made. I destroyed it and made a pitch. Everybody in my house was angry because Shabnam had gone to great trouble to grow a beautiful garden.

'After that, I made a gym upstairs, put lights on the pitch. Ashok Mankad was my mentor. I told him what I was doing with Yuvi, and he just nodded.

'When he had made me an opening batsman, he had said to me, "Yograj Singh, you have no idea how much potential you have. The problem is that there is no one to guide you."

'I wanted to do something different. International cricket is all about fast bowling, especially now, when we go abroad and encounter bouncy tracks. So I started with hard plastic and wet tennis balls. I remember that one day, we were practising in the backyard of our Chandigarh house. The ball went through the visor of Yuvi's helmet.

'Yuvi fell down and I remember that my mother yelled at me. She adored her grandson. I used to tell her, "You wait and watch, your grandson will become one of the greatest players ever." Unfortunately, she did not live long enough to see Yuvi become a great player. Shabnam reacted in much the same way. So many people used to comment on my practice sessions, which used to go on till late in the night and even during the cold days of winter.

'I believe that there is only one thing at the heart of discipline, devotion, dedication, all those big words, and that is hard work. No one should feel sorry for a person who works hard. I also believe that if you want to create something outstanding, you have to do something different to get there.

'At first it was very difficult for me to make Yuvi understand why I was doing it, why I was waking him up at six and making him play through the day. Today I think he realizes its value. Even if he doesn't, I don't want to comment on it. I believe that if you do anything, there should be a craziness, a madness for it. People called me mad but there was a method in the madness I pursued.

'As far as getting up in the morning was concerned, I have spent many years in your house, Makarand, and I remember you used to hit me very hard on my back to wake me up at 5 a.m. so that we could reach the venue for practice on time. We used to go by a crowded train from Andheri and, after playing the match, come back in the evening at eight, have a quick meal, and by ten, you would say, "Lights off! Go to sleep." So I think you will understand me.

'Yuvi reacted to the hard regimen I put him through in the same way as I reacted to you. There were times when I didn't like you because you were pushing me too hard. I used to ask myself why I had come back to cricket. But soon I realized that what you were doing was for my good. Why else would you have gone and recommended me to the national selectors when I had given up the game?

'Yuvi didn't realize it then and thought that his father was a Hitler. Even as an adult, he has made this statement: "I used to hate my father." I know he hated me. But somebody had to take the call.

'I always felt that something different had to be done. Yes, Yuvi was pushed hard for fitness, running twenty rounds at the age of eight. But I still believe that what I did was right. There were times when I had to break down the door and wake him up, pour a bucket of cold water on him. I once had to throw a tumbler full of milk at him. This may have been wrong in people's eyes, but today it has been proven that I was right.

'Of course, my mother and my wife were reacting to all this, and they weren't wrong. If they'd had a bat, they would have hit me on my head. But they didn't understand what I wanted to create. I think that when Yuvi was sixteen years old, he started realizing it himself, because he started enjoying his brilliance. He used to score 200, 250, and big hundreds.

'To cut the long story short, I want to say this. If Yuvi had just gone on with my training and had done all the things that his father had taught him to do in those twenty years, he would have scored 20,000 runs and maybe thirty internationals hundreds by now. He would never have got injured if he had listened to me. I believe fitness and training are the ultimate things in life, not only for a sportsman but for everybody: you, me or a five-year-old. We should aspire to be a sports-oriented family and a sports-oriented country. Like Australia.

'When Yuvi was sixteen, he was practising at the nets and Navjot Sidhu, captain of the Punjab Ranji team, saw him. He told me to include him in the Ranji team. Raj Singh Dungarpur said to me, "Ahh, a champion is here!" I said, "No, he is not ready yet." He said, "What are you talking about?" I said, "Sir, when he is ready, you'll know."

'Yuvi played his first Ranji Trophy match against Orissa and got out for a duck. For two and a half years after that, he didn't play Ranji. I think that Ranji match was a big mistake. An emotional decision made by Sidhu. Maybe he wanted to prove something to me or to Yuvi. Maybe he thought Yuvi had the potential to be a great player and he needed an opportunity. But I honestly felt that was a wrong decision.

'At the age of sixteen, Yuvi was concentrating on batting, lofting and hitting the ball cleanly. There were still a few things that had to be rectified. Also, there was the issue of fitness. It is different when you are playing U-14, U-16 and then U-19. When you are selected to play Ranji, you have to be ready for it. And I believe that you know you are ready when you are confident of handling pressure.

'By the time he was chosen for the U-19 World Cup team, Shabnam and I had separated. But Yuvi was with me during the U-19 World Cup and even during the ICC tournament in Nairobi. Soon after that, things started going wrong within the family. Yuvi left me. My mother had died. There was no one to hold him, no one to tell him to sleep at ten and wake up at five. He was treated like a star by his mother – mothers just can't be strict. And the limelight was on him at a very young age. It was very difficult for him to handle.

'I have my values. I am a man who loves and needs love. I cannot be pushed around by my wife, parents, son or anybody. Today Yuvi must realize that he has not done any good to himself by not coming to me. Whenever he did come to me in the past and wanted to have practice sessions, he enjoyed it. I made everything that he needed for good practice available to him.

'Perhaps his mother must have told him something about me, what I did when he was a child. And they must have struck a chord in his mind because they reminded him of how I had treated him during his making. Gradually we drifted apart. I felt bad, for I am the sort of person who would abandon the world for someone who came to me with love. But if someone walks away from me, or takes me for granted, I won't be there for them, regardless of who they are.

'Yuvi was born into such a great family, he could have done wonders by now if we hadn't been separated. Shouldn't he pity himself? For not being allowed to do what he is meant to be doing? Also, he should ask himself, has he been truthful to the game?

'I want to speak the bitter truth now. If you want to prepare someone for their future, three things have to be stopped immediately. One is the interference of relatives. Second, there has to be very strict discipline, even from the mother and grandmother, or whoever is living in the house. And there has to be one man who should take charge. This is very important and Yuvi should have done it himself, but I don't blame him because he thought what his father did with him was wrong. It wasn't Yuvi's fault at all. Everybody around him was saying the same thing.

'When he was eighteen, I told the media that Yuvi was the next Sobers. People laughed at me. Many ridiculed me. After those six sixes he hit in one over off Broad, the media wrote the same and Sobers endorsed it.

'I remember how it was when Yuvi made it to the U-19

World Cup team in 2000. To reach the U-19 took ten years and ten hours a day of preparation: batting, bowling and fielding. No television, no outings, no holidays. If he needed a friend, I was there. I was his friend, I was his mentor, I was his father, I was everything. Yes, I was ruthless, and you too, Makarand, used to get angry with me.

'But fitness is the most important thing. Even the great Sir Garfield Sobers once remarked to Bishen Singh Bedi that if he had known what fitness training was all about, he would have scored 50,000 runs!

'For me, fitness training meant running twenty or thirty rounds every day, sprinting 400 metres, taking 500 catches, gymming, four sessions of batting, and bowling. It was a ten-hour job. I would make him do six hours on the ground and then come back home and work for four hours more. And Makarand, you were a witness to it. There were times when you too felt that I was overdoing it.

'I think all this made Yuvi a better player. Also, he was the fittest. There was no one in the world except Jonty Rhodes who could match him as far as fielding was concerned.

'The point is not that you practise the whole day. It is how perfectly you practise. Yuvi was a brilliant left-arm fast bowler, and then he developed a lower back problem. Otherwise, we would have seen him bowl at 145 km per hour. That is what preparation is all about.

70

'If you want to get someone to be outstanding in this world, that is how you do it. You have to sacrifice so much. Your family, friends, everything. Only then will you achieve something in life. Look at Tiger Woods, Sunil Gavaskar, Sachin Tendulkar, Vivian Richards. Can we not learn from them?

'I am very unhappy about the progress Yuvraj has made as a cricketer. He has lived up to only 25 per cent of his ability and talent. The only person who has done justice to his talent is the great Sachin Ramesh Tendulkar. That is why I salute him all the time. He has been doing it day in and day out for the past twenty-three years. He has sacrificed so much for the country.

'Yuvi was not ready to listen to his father as far as cricket was concerned. He thought other people were better. Among the many things he has to learn is how to pace an innings. Don't throw away your wicket, I used to tell him. Score 200 not out, or 300 not out. Once, he scored 365 in the U-19 final against Bihar. I said, "Well played, well done, but you could have got 400 runs." His reply was, "Bacche ki jaan loge kya?" (Are you going to kill the boy now?). I said, "Don't talk to me like that again."

'Yuvi has so much power, such perfect timing, so much talent. He sights the ball so early that there is no need for him to hit sixes all the time. I used to tell him, "If I had ten per cent of your talent, I would have scored 100 and

200 in every alternate innings." Mahila Jayawardene and Kumara Sangakkara said this too.

'I used to tell him not to sweep the ball at the start, one should first know when to sweep. He needs to understand that it's not about deciding whether to play a stroke. It is knowing when and how to play a shot. "One has to visualize shot selection," I would say to him. But he used to brush me off. I wish I had played a hundred Test matches. Then maybe he would have listened to me.

'I have been taught by one of the best teachers in the cricketing circuit: Ashok Mankad. I think he is one of the greatest captains I played under, who took me from batting at number nine to opening the innings. It got me many hundreds. He always told me I didn't know my capability and where I was going wrong.

'Ashok Mankad made me practise my defence. Even today, if you want to succeed in Test cricket, you need to be a good defensive player. You must not throw your wicket away. It is not about hitting sixes and fours, it is about ones and twos and pacing your innings. Once, I remember, I got 136 runs against the Tatas and he shouted at me because I threw my wicket away.

'Yuvi should have realized this too. He could have come to his father and said, "Dad, one week with you. I am going to go and play a Test match." I would have said,

"Son, defence is very important, I am going to throw five hundred balls to you. You just defend. Front foot forward and defend the ball." But Yuvi was not prepared to listen to his father where cricket was concerned.

'What Yuvraj Singh is today is not his fault, it is the fault of the environment he has lived in. What is the use of having a lavish life, with cars and bungalows and money, if you are not doing the right things?

'He got carried away by the publicity and the glamour. He started playing to the gallery and not for himself. Yuvi became a superstar when they began to tell him, "Oh, you can hit a great six, you can hit it here or there!" There was a time when I used to tell him not to hit the ball because it wasn't possible to do so every time in international cricket. He would ask, "Then how do you get the runs?"

'Viv Richards used to say, "I am an entertainment man. I am here to entertain people." Fine, he could say that because he had achieved so much, he was the greatest. But if Yuvraj Singh starts saying that he is an entertainer, I am sorry, he has not reached that stage at all.

'I could compare Yuvi to Vinod Kambli. Such a great player. What happened to him? All the former Mumbai cricketers are responsible for what happened to Kambli. Nobody took him in hand, nobody mentored him.

'There were times when I used to give Yuvi a call and say, "Son, do this, do that", and he would say, "Yes, I'm doing it. I'm not a kid anymore". I used to feel so stupid. I would tell myself, Yograj Singh, why are you running after him? But I was doing it to ensure that his talent didn't go down the drain.

'Yuvi seems to have forgotten that all this glory is because of the game, because of this beautiful game called cricket. He has taken life for granted. Does he ever ask himself, What have I given back to the game? Is it enough to just go out and play?

'Because I was concerned about Yuvi's attitude, I once rang his mother, and she said, "Who the hell are you? You are a divorcee. Leave us alone." I talked to Yuvi, and the way he put me off, I felt deeply hurt.

'I think Yuvi's mother could have handled him better. He was only nineteen when he started playing international cricket. She seems to have pampered him. There was no one to question him. Does she ever stop him from going out, partying till late? Yuvi today doesn't know where he is going because he is surrounded by sycophants.

'Had I been there, I would have given him the stick. You may be a great player, but when you come home, you are a part of the family. You are Yuvraj Singh, you are not a star. I would have thrown him out of the house. Second,

74

I would have got him married to a wonderful girl who would have looked after the family and him.

'That's the reason he walked out on his father.

'Yuvi should have realized that he was born with a golden spoon. His dad gave him everything required to bring him to the highest level. He should have at least acknowledged that as far as cricket is concerned, he owes it to his father. Or he should have had the guts to tell his mother to let me do it my way. Things would have been very different. Even today, after his cancer, if he comes back and spends the rest of his life with me, I am sure you will see a different Yuvraj Singh because I can make things happen. I am a very, very disciplined and dedicated man.'

As he himself has often said, Yograj Singh never cared for or valued the opinion of others. Some call it confidence and some arrogance.

Yes, Yograj Singh has been extremely ruthless and unsympathetic and quite blind to his son's pain in the pursuit of his goal. I wonder, though: Isn't there a bit of Yograj in all of us? A father who desperately wants his son to follow his path. A father who wants to save his son from all the follies and mistakes that he himself committed.

Perhaps the only difference between an ordinary parent and Yograj is the extent of his determination. Behind the harsh taskmaster is the vulnerable heart of a father who cannot bear the thought of his talented son getting lost in obscurity. He preferred being hated for something worthwhile than being loved for nothing. He had to assume this role for the future of his son, in the hope that someday his son would come to him and say, 'Thank you, Dad, for making me'.

Yograj's vision has come true. Yuvraj Singh has made it and made it big. As for the father, his vision may have come true, but his dream still waits.

The author with young Yuvi in his Chandigarh house.

Newborn Yuvi in the arms of his grandfather

Yuvi with his younger brother Zorawar Singh

At the age of four

With his grandmother

At his father's film shooting location

In his grandmother's lap

With his father and grandmother

Skating at their Chandigarh house, with his grandmother in the background

On his way to six sixes in an over against England's Stuart Broad at the
Twenty20 World Championship in 2007

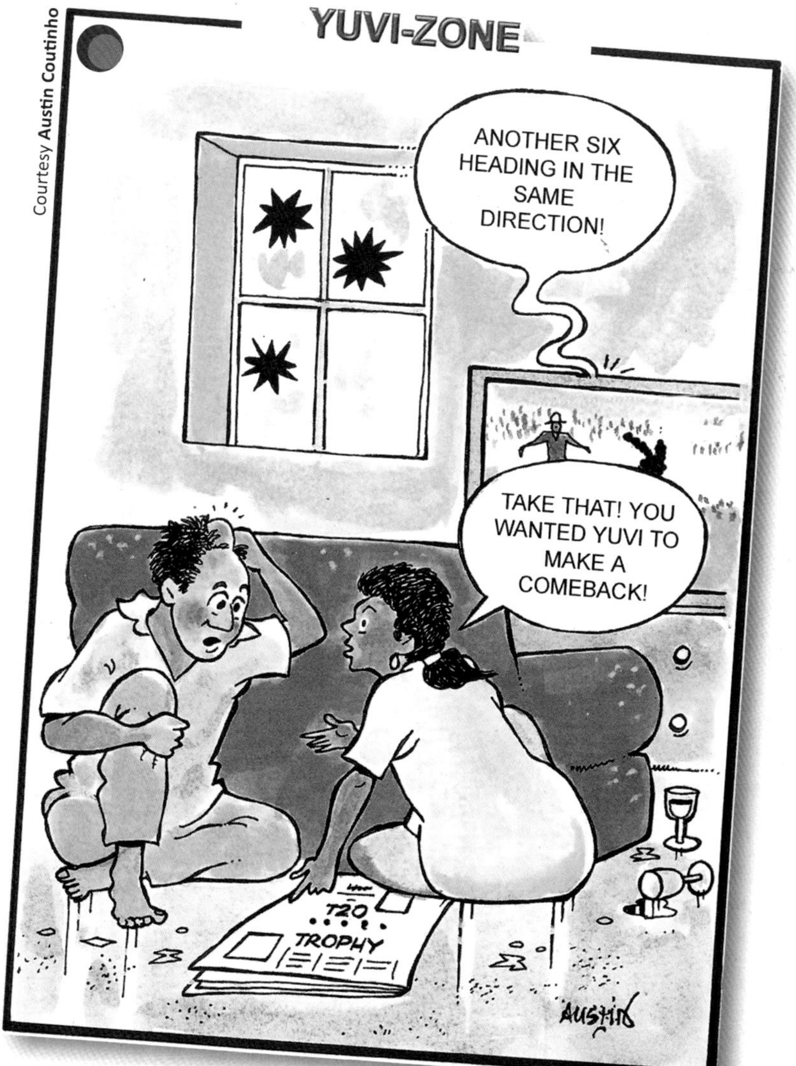

Courtesy **Austin Coutinho**

Celebrating as Shahid Afridi misses the stumps in a bowl off, giving victory to India after the match was tied during the ICC Twenty20 Cricket World Championship between India and Pakistan at Kingsmead on 14 September 2007 in Durban, South Africa.

Bat close to the body, defending the rising delivery on the backfoot against England during the fourth day of the second cricket test match at Trent Bridge in Nottingham, central England on 1 August 2011.

Bowling during the Cricket World Cup match between India and Ireland at the M. Chinnaswamy Stadium in Bangalore on 6 March 2011.

Rejoicing with the team after winning the final of the ICC World Cup 2011 against Sri Lanka at the Wankhede Stadium in Mumbai.

Posing with the ICC Cricket World Cup Trophy, the Gateway of India in the backdrop, on 3 April 2011 in Mumbai.

With the men in blue at a press conference after the World Cup win in 2011.
(LtoR) Yusuf Pathan, Harbhajan Singh, Mahendra Singh Dhoni, Yuvi and Piyush Chawla

ECAN

ANCER

.com

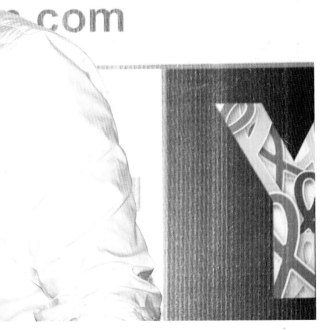

With his mother
Shabnam Singh at
a press conference
on 7 July 2012 in
New Delhi.

THE YU'VI'CTORY'

Chapter Six

Speaking of Technique

They say politicians never retire, they only fade away. This is true of cricketers too. Many try to continue their association with the game in some way or the other after retirement, but only a few have succeeded.

Most players do not think about or plan for their retirement when they are still playing top-level cricket, especially if they have been doing so for almost two decades. Sometimes a cricketer is forced to take a long break for health or injury reasons and it takes a tremendous effort to get back into form.

In Yuvi's case, it's not an ordinary injury or minor ailment that he has had to fight. Can he do it? Can he come back to play for India and compete with the best in the world? Certainly, no one is doubting his ability to fight the odds or the depth of his burning desire to return to the Indian team. So what will it take for Yuvi to make a significant comeback?

Cricket, like most sports, is played and won – or lost – in the mind. It takes a steadfast mind to handle the pressure, specially at the top level. That Yuvi never had any trouble handling pressure while he was fit is evident. But after such a long lay-off and treatment, he will have to iron out a few technical flaws in order to perform well in international cricket.

Former India captain Dilip Vengsarkar, a veteran of 116 Tests, has seen Yuvi play since he was sixteen. He says, 'Test cricket is different from any other format of the game. It's much tougher, and mentally and physically draining. Even the bowlers look to enhance their ratings and perform at their best. They make the batsman work hard for his runs by bowling accurately and giving nothing away. In ODIs, however, both bowlers and fielders are on the defensive, so it's easier for the batsman to play his shots.'

Vengsarkar should know. He was a naturally aggressive batsman who, as a teenager, hit E.A.S. Prasanna and Bishan

Bedi, two of India's top spinners, for seven towering sixes in a match between Rest of India and Bombay at Nagpur. But even he found it difficult to attack the bowling all the time, especially in first-class cricket. Polly Umrigar, a former India captain, advised Vengsarkar to spend more time in the middle if he wanted to succeed at the Test level. Vengsarkar immediately changed his approach and cut down on the lofted shots. He concentrated on playing more in the 'V' and went on to score sixteen Test centuries.

When batsmen in the earlier era encountered bowlers who were accurate, they preferred to be cautious. Mike Hendricks, the England fast bowler of the 1970s, was so confident of not bowling a single half volley that he once promised to buy a round of lager for his county colleagues if he ever bowled one! There were many like Hendricks, who were so accurate that it was difficult for batsmen to attack them. Today's players, however, do not accept this strategy.

Yuvi, for instance, is essentially a front foot player. He is so good at driving the ball through the off side that bowlers tempt him by bowling around the off stump. Sometimes the batsman is likely to misjudge the length and if he doesn't know his off stump, he is in for trouble, as Yuvi has found out far too often.

Analysing the technical aspects of Yuvi's game, Saad Bin Jung, nephew of Tiger Pataudi and a former Hyderabad opener who, at the age of seventeen, scored a scintillating hundred for South Zone in 1978 against the likes of Malcolm Marshall and Vanburn Holder without wearing a helmet, says, 'Yuvi has great hand-eye coordination and today he is the greatest batsman that we have. On his day many of us rate his talent as high as any other Indian player's, if not higher, though he is different from our other greats in one unique way. He is tall and strong and has the gift of exceptional timing and he flexes his body more than any other when he bats, using more muscle and whip than a normal batsman would. This on a good day gives him an edge over the greatest of them all and on his off day makes him more ordinary than the average. That's why the inconsistency in his batting performance. The advantage with having Yuvi in the side is that even before he goes in to bat, say in a T20 game, he is at least 20 runs plus, these being runs saved by his brilliance in the field, and when he fails with the bat he makes up for it with the ball.

'Yuvi bats with an unduly high back lift and though this is where he gets his strength from, it's also his Achilles' heel. In order to keep the ball down, a batsman with a shorter back lift is pushed hard when he has to play the square cut and hook as he is forced to take the bat above the ball in order to keep the ball down. A high back lift overcomes this deficiency with ease and that's why you will find that batsmen like Yuvi with a higher back lift are much better while playing square off the wicket. At any given time, his bat is looking down on the ball and this opens up the entire field for him. Though the high back lift helps him deliver greater impetus, it tends to lead to a looser game. Because of the extra distance the bat has to travel to meet the normal good length ball, the batsman needs to commit himself that fraction of a second earlier than usual. This can become a big disadvantage when he is playing truly quick bowling or genuine seam. Not only does he have to commit early but once committed, he finds it very difficult to change his shot as the momentum at the downswing of the bat is greater than that of a normal batsman. Further, as the bat has to perform a larger arc, even the slightest error in the downswing is greatly enhanced by the time the bat meets the ball, resulting in the risk of the bat coming across the ball. When this happens, it appears that Yuvi is playing a loose shot although in reality he is only doing what he knows best: playing cricket the only way he knows how to, sometimes like a genius and sometimes like any of us.'

Saad adds, 'Most times, good seam bowlers on average tracks get murdered by him but if the wicket assists seam, then the intelligent bowlers exploit this disadvantage. A batsman who is technically challenged has to be really good with his timing. On his day, when he is moving well, he is a treat to watch. If you watch the footage of Viv Richards playing and analyse how he batted, you can see that he controlled and varied his back lift to meet that particular shot. His genius lay in optimizing his back lift, yet generating the amazing power that he did. That's why Richards was so consistent. Complete control at all times is the hallmark of all great players. To me, Yuvi on his day is as great a player as Viv Richards.'

Like Yuvi, the well-known Australian batsman Michael Bevan, too, was brilliant in ODIs but failed miserably in Tests. He just couldn't adapt to the line and length he faced from the bowler. At first he did not believe he had a problem. But when it kept happening innings after innings, it got to him. The more he thought about it, the more he discussed it, the more pressure he ended up putting on himself, until the problem became psychological rather than technical. Bevan scored 785 in 18 Tests at an average of 29.07, whereas in 232 ODIs he scored 6912 runs at 53.58 and also won some amazing matches on his own. Compare his figures with those of Yuvi who, in 35 Tests scored 1775 runs at an average of 34.80 but in 274 ODIs scored 8051 runs with an average of 37.62. Bevan remained not out on 67 occasions. Perhaps he focussed too much on the short ball solution. But when he acknowledged that the short ball was a real problem, he tried to do something about it. Yuvi, unfortunately, feels he does not have a problem.

Greg Chappell, who has studied the game of both Bevan and Yuvi, says, 'Yuvi and Michael Bevan are very similar players. They make ODI cricket look simple, but neither has been able to adjust to the longer format. Both had difficulties with pace, especially when it was delivered between chest and head with catching fielders close to the bat. I have no doubt that had they come to grips with the mental aspects of this, they could both have been successful at Test cricket.

'Why they were able to overcome their doubts in ODIs is that often the field was back by the time they came to the wicket and it was harder for opposition teams to bowl their best fast bowlers for long periods. Both were great finishers in ODI cricket and most teams would be happy to have them in their line-up. And the combination of Yuvi and Dhoni was almost unbeatable.'

Here Greg Chappell is spot on. Psychology plays a very crucial role. If a player is unwilling to make the adjustments demanded by the longer format, his performance cannot improve.

Vengsarkar, who himself loved playing the hook shot, analyses Yuvi's technique against short stuff. 'I guess the problem is his initial front foot movement. He will be okay if he sorts out the initial movement (just before the ball is delivered). He has to keep his head as steady as possible while facing fast bowlers, and try and remain side on all the time. Practising against short-pitched deliveries with tennis balls might help too.'

At the international level, rival team managements provide their players with vital technical inputs, and they practise according to a plan. In the case of Yuvi, the strategy they adopt is to test him against the short stuff, push him on the back foot and then mix it with deliveries around off stump which tempt him to drive. He gets away with it on subcontinent pitches, but in Test matches, on tracks that afford bounce and lateral movement, he struggles when faced with bowling which has pace. The other issue is the consequence of his being a wristy player. Whenever a player uses more wrist to deliver added force, he is in danger of getting out if he makes even the slightest error in timing. Also, while playing the quickies, the inherent urge to go chest on has to be controlled at all times. The fact that Yuvi squares up every now and then is because of a combination of the facts discussed above. Whenever a batsman gets into a bad trot, there are a few things he does: he drops his back lift till he starts to get back his feel, he starts to play in the V, he starts to focus more on the bottom hand, keeping the face of the bottom hand in the direction of the shot and holding his elbow out, thereby forcing himself to lock into a side on position. One of the areas that batsmen err in consistently is the placement of their toes. Time and again, we have observed Yuvi fall prey to this small but crucial slip. When playing back, if the back toe faces cover, it naturally forces the body to square up, and in order to play through cover, the batsman has to compensate and correct his downswing. He starts to play inside out to a ball he should be playing straight.

Another factor that needs to be emphasized is the advent of the helmet in the sport. As Saad Bin Jung says, 'A player with a helmet starts to close his eyes while one without a helmet keeps them open at all times and watches the ball right through. And that's why it's absolutely necessary, keeping in mind that every Indian batsman has a similar problem with the short-pitched delivery, that we try and find out if we are making a mistake during early training. Sunil Gavaskar, Viv Richards, Barry Richards, Rohan Kanhai, Vijay Manjrekar, G.R. Vishwanath, to name a few, learnt their game and moulded their instincts into technique without a helmet. Ganguly, Tendulkar, Dravid, Yuvraj, Raina, Kohli did it with a helmet. This is where the problem lies. Maybe proper technique can only be inculcated without the helmet.'

The former Mumbai opener Zubin Bharucha, who scored a hundred on debut for Mumbai in both the Irani Trophy and the Ranji Trophy, and is at present coach of the Rajasthan Royals, analyses Yuvi's game very well. He says that when he was invited by Yograj Singh to Chandigarh to work with Yuvi for a few days, a couple of things struck him about the young man. One was his ability to learn something quickly and adapt it, the other his stunning talent of striking a cricket ball as cleanly as one might ever see, the only other person with similar purity of strike being the young Sachin Tendulkar.

'At that time, when I evaluated his technique, I observed that there was minimal on-side play. One of the things I was keen on achieving on that trip was to get him to score more runs between mid-on and fine-leg. He understood the importance of the same and quickly adapted his foot position as well as the follow through movement. No cricketing manual will tell you this, but all great on-side players know that when one plays on the on-side, it is important to fall over with the back leg coming through in front of the body. He picked up the movement and immediately started using it. I truly believe there are only a few minor tweaks, especially with the feet and downswing, required for him to go on and become a successful Test player at number five for India.

'It's actually a problem common to quite a few Indian batsmen: the commitment of the front foot early and across the body. This becomes fatal when one misjudges length, and it's something which happens with regular frequency, as it's part and parcel of batting. After you commit that front foot forward and realize the ball is a little short, you withdraw it, and that's the biggest error you can make, because it means you are taking the foot and head away from the line of the ball and, as a result, will have no option but to hang the bat outside the body. And this, as we all know, has disastrous results, as now you are only presenting half a bat to the ball and will, more often than not, end up nicking it.'

Bharucha adds, 'A number of present-day Indian batsmen like Suresh Raina, Rohit Sharma and Gautam Gambhir also suffer from this initial front foot movement. This is no fault of theirs, it's simply driven by the conditions in which one has learnt one's cricket, the result of having been brought up playing on low, and slow, wickets. Of course, one could always question the quality of instruction available, as opposed to blaming the cricketer. However, a few sessions focussed on understanding the repercussions of their actions can easily solve the problem, as these guys are all amazingly talented.

'Virat Kohli, too, does it occasionally, but gets away with it at times because of standing further towards leg stump, which helps him get the bat down on a better plane, i.e., "over middle stump" more often than not, as opposed to it coming down outside off stump, which it would be if you stand on middle stump – this only exacerbates caught behind and LBW dismissals.'

Kapil Dev, one of the great natural all-rounders the game has known, has a simple philosophy. He believes that no cricketer must overload the body. 'Initially, when I was young, I was bowling quick, but later when Sunil Gavaskar explained to me that as a main bowler I would be required to bowl 25 overs per innings, I learnt to bowl within my capability. But in batting, I didn't restrain myself. I think Yuvi must learn to adapt himself to Test cricket. When the going is good, he looks great but when he struggles, he looks pathetic. You can't expect him to score centuries all the time, but he is capable of doing much better in Test matches than he has done so far.' The philosophy that Kapil Dev advocates is simple, but one must emphasize that to succeed at the top, that is, in Test cricket, one's basic technique has to be impeccable.

What next for Yuvi, is the question. To get back to international cricket, he will have to be hundred per cent fit and play consistently well in domestic tournaments. No selection committee will risk selecting a player on past performance, especially while he is recovering from a serious illness. Renowned sports psychologist Dr Rudi Webster, who handled the West Indies team in their heyday, says, 'Yuvi is now on the road to recovery following his successful chemotherapy sessions in the US. His recovery will not be all smooth sailing. He will have his ups and downs, and will have to deal with testing emotional challenges because recovery hardly ever follows a straight and steady path.

'Yuvraj's mental state will be critical in his healing because the proper use of his mind will enable him to stimulate the healing powers that are already within him. For centuries, yogis have been telling us about these powers. Today, two new fields of science substantiate their claims – signal transduction and epigenetics. These fields have shown how our mind and the perception of our environment can select, modify and regulate the activity of our genes and the fate of the trillions of cells in our body, particularly their function, survival and even their death. They have shown how our genes are constantly being remoulded by life's experiences and by our perception and interpretation of those experiences.

'Yuvraj will change the path and trajectory of his recovery if he changes his outlook and gets rid of the limiting beliefs and the negative thoughts and pictures that come to the fore in situations like his. The thoughts and pictures that he imprints in his mind today will determine what he becomes tomorrow.

'He should also build a positive and supportive network of friends and supporters to help him create the right healing environment with humour, laughter, cheerfulness being a part of it.

'Instead of focussing on what has been and on what he fears, he should concentrate on what he wants to see happen and what he wants to become. Every day, he should create and constantly replay images of himself as a healthy, kind and loving person. And he should imagine himself representing his country again with distinction. The more he replays these images, the quicker he will heal. His brain will not just create these images; it will do everything in its power to make them a reality.'

Once you start playing international cricket, there is a fine line between natural ability and technique. If one has the basics in place, one's natural abilities will help to combat difficult situations. Yuvraj Singh, like many other natural stroke players, is a treat to watch when he in the zone, but he has shown himself to be inadequate when it comes to technical perfection.

Chapter Seven

CLIMBING THE PEAK

For four years, Rafael Nadal remained the second-best tennis player in the world. For four long years, he tried his best to upset Roger Federer, the World No. 1, from his position, but he couldn't. Then one fine Wimbledon afternoon, Nadal rose and shone and there he was, the champion. Finally.

How did it happen? What did Nadal do this time that changed the course of his life? What inspired him to perform so brilliantly? Will we ever know what brought it about?

Similarly, how do we try and understand what triggered that sparkling performance from Yuvraj Singh when he almost single-handedly took India to victory in the World Cup in 2011? What was it that made someone who had been playing for India for a decade, and had been a part of three World Cups and numerous other World Championships, click at just the right moment?

There was enormous pressure as the tournament was being held at home and India's reputation was at stake. But right from the start of the tournament, Yuvi had seemed different from his usual self. The restlessness was missing. There was an air of tranquillity about him. He was calm and confident, as if he had suddenly become a mature and thinking player, who would play percentage cricket after reading the situation. He seemed to have realized that bowlers did not step on to the ground to allow batsmen to take liberties with them.

Besides, this was a golden opportunity for him to silence his detractors. Did he want to prove something to them, to all those who had been critical of him, accusing him of concentrating more on off-the-field activities than his performance on the ground? Was that his motivation? All Yuvi said was that he wanted to win the World Cup for one special person. Was it for Sachin Tendulkar that Yuvi gave his all? Or had Yuvi realized his past mistakes and was desirous of correcting them? Was there something more to the story that we don't know? What made Yuvi so confident of winning the World Cup?

Positive thinking is often evident in good players before big events, but being so completely self-assured is a different thing. It speaks of something else. An inner struggle or an inner realization, perhaps. Analysts of the game can offer conjectures, fans can make predictions and the media can sensationalize events as much as they like, but they cannot provide the truth. Only an insider who knows the player and the situation can explain such a turnaround. And one such person is Ranjib Biswal, manager of the Indian team. He and Ramji Srinivasan, who trained the team, enjoyed a close relationship with the players and were privy to what went on in the dressing room.

Ranjib Biswal had captained the India U-19 team in 1988–89 in four Test matches against Pakistan in India. He went on to become an administrator and is currently President of the Odisha Cricket Association. As a national selector, Biswal represented East Zone and served under Kiran More, Dilip Vengsarkar and K. Srikkanth. In 2006, he was appointed manager of the Indian team for a tour of the West Indies.

Biswal explained that his relationship with the players was not limited to his managerial role. 'The whole team was like a family,' he says.

Biswal had watched Yuvi closely before and during the World Cup. In fact, he has followed Yuvi's career over the last five years and is in the best position to comment on his state of mind at the time and to provide some insights into the enigma that is Yuvraj Singh.

In 2011 the stage was set for the biggest tournament ever: the World Cup. Cricket was back in the prime-time slot on most news channels. The high decibel levels of the anchors in TV studios matched the excitement of fans outside. The question on all lips was, 'Will India do it this time?' The emphasis was undoubtedly on 'this time'. Every five minutes, a photograph of Kapil Dev in the balcony at Lord's, celebrating the 1983 win, appeared on the screen with some competition from images of the 2007 T20 win.

Prayers, discussions, debates, speculation, the country had done it all. Finally, satisfied that they had played their part and sung enough songs, painted their faces suitably and drunk adequate quantities of sponsored cold drinks for the team to be motivated, they sat back and waited for the payback from their millionaire cricketers.

In the dressing room, the atmosphere was more tense than anyone could imagine. Here were the fifteen players who actually had to slog it out and fulfil the expectations of a billion fans, turn their dream into reality by winning the

World Cup. They had to overpower fourteen international teams before they could hold the Cup in their hands. And only one of the over 200 internationally admired players would be declared Man of the Tournament.

India won the Cup, and an Indian cricketer was awarded the most coveted prize. Who would have thought that he had played the entire series with a deadly cancer growing in his system?

Manager Ranjib Biswal clearly remembers noticing that something was wrong with Yuvi's health during the World Cup. 'But since we are not doctors, we did not know how seriously to take it,' he says. 'He was falling sick on and off. He felt nauseous and vomited frequently. Sometimes he used to get breathless. He complained of a stiff neck. But the physio was taking care of him, and no one thought it was a serious illness. We thought he should get a proper check-up after the World Cup was over. In fact, I remember N. Srinivasan, who was then secretary and now president of the BCCI, telling me that after the World Cup Yuvi needed to get a complete check-up done because he was clearly not well. No one ever thought that it would be cancer.'

The World Cup stretched over fifty-six days but since there were four or five days off between matches, Yuvi managed to recover in time for each match. 'During the

World Cup, we tried to manage his physical fitness with the help of physios so that he would not break down in the middle of the series,' Biswal says.

In the early phases of his career, illness and injury would set Yuvi back for quite a long time. But this time, sickness didn't deter him at all. It was as if his poisoned insides were giving him greater inspiration and pressed him to try harder. 'One thing I noticed about Yuvi in this World Cup was that he was more determined. I think it was because he was coming back after a poor series in South Africa and Sri Lanka. His place in the team was being challenged by Raina and Jadeja. That pressure was enough to get him motivated. He spent long hours in the nets, bowling and then working on his fielding with the coach. Even when there was optional practice, Yuvi would be present. And slowly, after the first match, he started doing well. He started concentrating more on his bowling as well. Gary Kirsten and the others were supportive of him because everyone knew that if Yuvi clicked, it was going to be much easier for us to win the World Cup.'

Yuvi's skills as a bowler had long been recognized and he was called upon regularly, at least in One-day Internationals. He was used quite extensively in the latter half of the series against Sri Lanka in July 2010. Before the World Cup, Yuvi took up bowling very seriously. He knew he was a key member of the team, an all-rounder who had to contribute with both bat and ball. The game-plan for the World Cup had been chalked out well in advance. 'And Yuvi was the right choice to fit the number six slot as an all-rounder,' says Biswal. 'He already had a tremendous ability with the bat; his bowling became an added advantage.'

That Yuvi was determined to put in a sterling performance during the tournament was obvious. 'During the warm up, or the practice football sessions earlier, you could see Yuvi giving his hundred per cent. Even when it came to training with Ramji, Yuvi was meticulous. He never missed a single session. Nor did he miss any nets. The intensity that I saw in Yuvi then was different from what I had seen on any other tour I had been on with him.'

According to Ramji Srinivasan, the planning and training for the World Cup had started in 2010 itself in Sri Lanka, and Yuvi had shown extraordinary energy since then. 'Yuvi, as usual, was very determined. There was nothing noticeable while he was training during the World Cup. He used to cough, but we didn't think it was serious. He was doing all the work in the gym, SAQ [speed, agility and quickness], speed endurance work, Core, etc., in addition to his specialized fitness workout of at least five sessions a week.

'Ranjib Biswal is spot on when he says that there was a look of fortitude in Yuvi's eyes. One instance I would definitely like to highlight is his speed endurance work in Sri Lanka during our tour of 2010. We had speed endurance sessions after the day's play. I still have the sets, reps, time, and the distance he covered during one of the sessions. Munaf Patel was at a great fitness level and was giving Yuvi company in his training. Being a pace bowler, Munaf's workout schedule was much harder than Yuvi's, but Yuvi was determined to do the session with Munaf. The workout was of a very high intensity, and Yuvi defied nausea and completed the course. He was floored after the workout but the point was that he finished it fully and effectively. I was stunned and my respect for him grew dramatically. That day I understood that his will to win was greater than his fear of failure. It left me with a feeling of awe and deep satisfaction.'

Having watched Yuvi from his U-19 days, Ramji recognizes that he is a fighter. Coming back to the training for the World Cup, he says, 'It was specialized, and not like the generalized stuff they did prior to the World Cup. Specialized training need not be physically hard but it can be technically challenging. I am sure Yuvi was unaware of his medical condition. But sometimes ignorance is indeed bliss. And not knowing the real cause and effect of his condition put less pressure on him.'

Cricket is played more in the mind, and in extremely competitive situations like the World Cup, one's state of mind becomes the key factor in one's performance. Yuvi's composure at this juncture must have played a significant role in his performance on the ground.

Perhaps looking for reasons to explain the change in Yuvi during the World Cup is a futile exercise. The only person who can provide the answers is Yuvi himself, though it's equally likely that he is not entirely aware of them either. Not all decisions are made after chalking out a logical step-by-step flowchart. And not all actions and changes are the consequence of a particular cause. You just feel a pull from life and you allow yourself to get dragged along. This might have happened to Yuvi too. Be that as it may, what is obvious is that something in Yuvi had indeed changed, to allow him to put in a charged performance, such as had rarely been seen before.

Chapter Eight

THE FUTURE BECKONS

One thing is clear about Yuvi: he has courage, resilience and an undaunted fighting spirit. How could someone play and excel in the World Cup while being so dangerously unwell, is a question to which nobody has an answer.

And now that Yuvi is back on the field, how long will he take to establish himself in the Test side? To any cricketer, the number of Test matches he plays is more important than the number of pyjama cricket matches. How could Yuvi be an exception? At the end of a player's career, it's the number of Test matches he has played that matter. That's what decides the worth of a cricketer.

It's not that Yuvi doesn't have the skills required to be a world-class Test cricketer. All he has to do is focus on Test matches, and the rest of the formats will be a cinch. As Sir Garfield Sobers said during his playing days, 'The difference between a great player and a good player is that the great player rarely commits the same mistake twice and is always precise with shot selection. Good players tend to repeat the same mistake several times.'

Yuvi should get enough motivation by watching old footage of those two great left-handers, Sobers and Brian Lara. While Yuvi isn't far behind in stroke play, it is in execution that he needs to put in a more meaningful effort. Nobody expects him to grind the bowlers. That was never his game and that is not going to be his game. At the same time, he must know that international bowlers are unlikely to give him any quarter because of his recent illness. They are armed with information and analyses, and they plan and execute their moves ruthlessly.

In the 1977–78 tour of Australia, Jimmy Amarnath was hit on the head by a bouncer from Jeff Thompson – those were the days when helmets didn't exist. He fell and got up again and faced another bouncer. The attack became more fierce, and with no limit on the number of bouncers, Thompson kept bouncing him and Amarnath kept hooking.

Bishan Bedi, the skipper of that team, told me, 'Even after Jimmy was hit on the head, he kept hooking, and that too on the bouncy Perth wicket. Never have I seen a more courageous batsman. Jimmy never ever ducked. He was getting hit, but he never flinched.'

If Yuvi reworks his approach to the game, like many others have done after reaching the wrong side of thirty, he can still be devastating. He has been playing international cricket for more than a decade. He has made a tremendous impact on international cricket, especially with his six sixes in the 2007 T20 World Championship. But does he want his fans all over the world to remember the man who hit Stuart Broad all over the park, or the man who scored a brilliant match-winning century against South Africa's deadly fast bowlers on their soil in a Test match?

Time and again, Yuvi has said that he wants to say goodbye to the game after playing a minimum of hundred Tests. He has played 37, and there are 63 to go. It's true that because of a packed middle order in the Indian team, he hasn't been able to cement his place in the Test side. But now that he is the most experienced middle-order batsman other than Sachin Tendulkar, all he has to do is spend more time with Tendulkar and learn as much as he can from him.

Yuvi is the same age in 2012 that Tendulkar was in 2003. He has shared a dressing room with him, chatted with him and eaten with him. Didn't Tendulkar go through hell with potentially career-ending injuries? How has he managed to stage a comeback? Yuvi witnessed that too.

The Duncan Fletcher formula of batting that has been praised by several former England batsmen may perhaps help him sort out a few technical issues. If the formula could help Michael Vaughan and Nasser Hussain, it can also help Yuvi fine-tune his technique.

Yuvi has a minimum of five years of cricket left in him, provided he does what an international cricketer needs to do – stay focussed. Money and fame cease to be motivating factors at some stage in one's life. What one then strives for is stature that is permanent and cannot be tarnished.

Yuvi has enough time to get there. And more than enough motivation and skill. I have no doubt that with the kind of hard work and diligence he is capable of, he will finally achieve what he so dearly wants – an immortal place in the history of the game he loves so much and has given so much of himself to.

YUVRAJ SINGH: THE FIGURES

(b. 12 December 1981, Chandigarh) LHB LM

RANJI TROPHY FOR PUNJAB

(debut for Punjab v Orissa at Punjab Cricket Association Stadium in Mohali, 7–10 February 1997)

Season	Opponent	M	I	No	Runs	HS	Ave	100	50	0	CT	B	M	Runs	Wkt	Ave	5s	10s	B/B	Captaincy			
																				W	L	Dr	To
1996–97	Orissa	1	1	0	0	0	0.00	0	0	1	0	6	0	7	0	0.00	0	0		Played as an opener and scored 0 on debut			
1997–98	Did not participate																						
1998–99	Hyderabad	1	2	0	38	20	19.00	0	0	0	2	42	0	15	0	0.00	0	0					
1999–00	Del, Hary, Hyd, Baro, Bihar, Rail, TN	7	10	1	397	149	44.11	1	2	1	1	120	5	67	2	33.50	0	0	1/5				
2000–01	Del, Raj, Mum	3	5	0	214	135	42.80	1	0	0	5	24	0	23	1	23.00	0	0	1/18				
2001–02	HP, Serv, J&K, Hary, Del, Ass, Ori, Baro	8	14	0	593	109	42.36	2	4	2	14	222	12	66	3	22.00	0	0	3/25	0	0	1	1
2002–03	Did not participate																						

Courtesy: Sudhir Vaidya

Season	Opponent	M	I	No	Runs	HS	Ave	100	50	0	CT	B	M	Runs	Wkt	Ave	5s	10s	B/B	Captaincy			
																				W	L	Dr	To
2003–04	Del, Rail, Kerala	3	3	0	256	138	85.33	1	1	0	3	–	–	–	–	–	–	–					
2004–05	UP, Ass, Baro, Maha, TN, Mum	6	9	1	250	66	31.25	0	2	2	5	36	1	24	0	0.00	0	0					
2005–06	Did not participate																						
2006–07	Did not participate																						
2007–08	Did not participate																						
2008–09	Delhi	1	2	0	38	38	19.00	0	0	1	1	60	0	25	1	25.00	0	0	1/25				
2009–10	Did not participate																						
2010–11	UP, Karn, HP	3	6	0	313	92	52.17	0	3	0	0	156	4	91	1	91.00	0	0	1/59				
2011–12	Did not participate																						
TOTAL		**33**	**52**	**2**	**2099**	**149**	**41.98**	**5**	**12**	**7**	**31**	**666**	**22**	**318**	**8**	**39.75**	**0**	**0**	**3/25**	**0**	**0**	**1**	**1**

Highest score in Ranji Trophy: 149 v Haryana at Nehru Stadium, Gurgaon, 1999–00

DULEEP TROPHY FOR NORTH ZONE

Season	Opponent	M	I	No	Runs	HS	Ave	100	50	0	CT	B	M	Runs	Wkt	Ave	5s	10s	B/B	Captaincy			
																				W	L	Dr	To
2000–01	South, West, East, Central	4	7	1	346	130	57.67	1	2	0	5	12	1	1	0	0.00	0	0					
2001–02	South	1	1	0	209	209	209.00	1	0	0	0	–	–	–	–	–	–	–					
2002–03	Did not participate																						
2003–04	Central, East	2	4	0	305	148	76.25	2	0	0	4	–	–	–	–	–	–	–					
2004–05	West, South	2	4	2	291	110	145.50	2	1	0	2	–	–	–	–	–	–	–					
	TOTAL	9	16	3	1151	149	88.54	6	3	0	11	12	1	1	0	0.00	0	0					

Highest score in Duleep Trophy: 209 v South Zone at Nahar Singh Stadium, Faridabad, 2001–02

IRANI CUP ALL FOR REST OF INDIA

Season	Opponent	M	I	NO	Runs	HS	Ave	100	50	0	CT	B	M	Runs	Wkt	Ave	5s	10s	B/B	Captaincy			
																				W	L	Dr	To
2002–03	for Rest v Railways at Delhi	1	2	0	76	50	38.00	0	1	0	0	48	3	26	0	0.00	0	0					
2003–04	for Rest v Mumbai at Chennai	1	2	0	32	27	16.00	0	0	0	1	–	–	–	–	–	–	–					
2010–11	for Rest v Mumbai at Jaipur	1	2	1	208	204 *	208.00	1	0	0	3	12	0	5	0	0.00	0	0		1	0	0	1
	TOTAL	3	6	1	316	204 *	63.20	1	1	0	4	60	3	31	0	0.00	0	0		1	0	0	1

Highest score in Irani Cup: 204 (n o) for Rest of India v Mumbai at Sawai Mansingh Stadium, Jaipur in 2010–11

TESTS

(debut v New Zealand at Punjab Cricket Association Stadium in Mohali, 16–20 October 2003 – Test Cap No. 247)

Season	Opponent	M	I	No	Runs	HS	Ave	100	50	0	CT	B	M	Runs	Wkt	Ave	5s	10s	B/B	Captaincy			
																				W	L	Dr	To
2003–04	New Zealand in India	1	2	1	25	20	25.00	0	0	0	0	6	0	1	0	0.00	0	0					
2003–04	Pakistan in Pakistan	3	4	0	230	112	57.50	1	1	0	2	54	0	32	1	32.00	0	0	1/25				
2004–05	Australia in India	2	4	1	47	27	15.67	0	0	0	6	24	0	10	0	0.00	0	0					
2005–06	Zimbabwe in Zimbabwe	2	2	0	37	25	18.50	0	0	0	1	–	–	–	–	–	–	–					
2005–06	Sri Lanka in India	2	4	1	152	77*	50.67	0	2	2	0	–	–	–	–	–	–	–					
2005–06	Pakistan in Pakistan	3	3	0	171	122	57.00	1	0	0	4	54	0	46	0	0.00	0	0					
2005–06	England in India	2	3	0	64	37	21.33	0	0	0	1	–	–	–	–	–	–	–					

Season	Opponent	M	I	No	Runs	HS	Ave	100	50	0	CT	B	M	Runs	Wkt	Ave	5s	10s	B/B	Captaincy			
																				W	L	Dr	To
2005–06	West Indies in West Indies	4	7	1	104	39	17.33	0	0	1	7	6	0	1	0	0.00	0	0					
2007–08	Pakistan in India	1	2	0	171	169	85.50	1	0	0	1	54	2	20	2	10.00	0	0	2/9				
2007–08	Australia in Australia	2	4	0	17	12	4.25	0	0	2	1	12	0	11	0	0.00	0	0					
2007–08	South Africa in India	1	1	0	32	32	32.00	0	0	0	0	72	1	46	1	46.00	0	0	1/39				
2008–09	England in India	2	4	1	212	86	70.67	0	2	0	1	144	4	65	2	32.50	0	0	1/12				
2008–09	New Zealand in New Zealand	3	5	1	125	54 *	31.25	0	1	1	2	135	2	84	1	84.00	0	0	1/11				
2009–10	Sri Lanka in India	3	3	0	158	68	52.67	0	2	0	1	138	1	90	1	90.00	0	0	1/7				
2009–10	Bangladesh in Bangladesh	2	2	0	37	25	18.50	0	0	0	2	52	2	25	0	0.00	0	0					

Season	Opponent	M	I	No	Runs	HS	Ave	100	50	0	CT	B	M	Runs	Wkt	Ave	5s	10s	B/B	Captaincy			
																				W	L	Dr	To
2010	Sri Lanka in Sri Lanka	1	2	0	57	52	28.50	0	1	0	0	–	–	–	–	–	–	–					
2011	England in England	1	2	0	70	62	35.00	0	1	0	1	72	0	52	1	52.00	0	0	1/51				
2011–12	West Indies in India	2	3	0	66	25	22.00	0	0	0	0	30	0	18	0	0	0	0					
	TOTAL	37	57	6	1775	169	34.80	3	10	6	31	853	12	501	9	55.67	0	0	2/9				

Highest score in Tests: 169 in the 3rd Test v Pakistan at M. Chinnaswamy Stadium, Bengaluru, 2007–08

OTHER FIRST-CLASS MATCHES

Season	Opponent	M	I	No	Runs	HS	Ave	100	50	0	CT	B	M	Runs	Wkt	Ave	5s	10s	B/B	Captaincy			
																				W	L	Dr	To
2001–02	India 'A' v South Africa 'A' at Bloemfontein	2	3	0	186	107	62.00	1	1	0	2	30	0	24	0	0	0	0					
2003	For Yorkshire in County Cricket Championship in England	7	12	2	145	56	14.50	0	2	0	12	207	5	130	3	43.33	0	0					
2003–04	For Board President's XI v New Zealand	1	1	1	80	80*	–	0	1	0	0	–	–	–	–	–	–	–	1/8				
2007	India in England	3	6	2	162	59	40.50	0	1	0	1	180	3	118	0	0	0	0					
2007–08	Indians v Victoria in Australia	1	1	1	6	6*	–	0	0	0	0	–	–	–	–	–	–	–					
2008–09	Board President's XI v Australia at Hyderabad	1	2	0	142	113	71.00	1	0	0	1	69	3	19	1	19.00	0	0	1/9				

Season	Opponent	M	I	No	Runs	HS	Ave	100	50	0	CT	B	M	Runs	Wkt	Ave	5s	10s	B/B	Captaincy		
																				W	L	Dr	To
2010	Indians v S L Board President XI at Colombo (Colts) in Sri Lanka	1	1	0	118	118	118.00	1	0	0	0	6	0	11	0	0		0				
2011	Indians v Somerset in England	1	1	0	0	0	0.00	0	0	1	1	60	0	76	0	0	0	0				
	TOTAL	**17**	**27**	**6**	**839**	**118**	**39.95**	**3**	**5**	**1**	**17**	**552**	**11**	**378**	**4**	**94.50**	**0**	**0**	**1/8**	**0**	**0**	**0**	**0**

Highest score in other first-class cricket matches: 118 v Sri Lanka Board President's XI at Colombo in Sri Lanka, 2010

COMPREHENSIVE TOTAL – FIRST-CLASS CRICKET MATCHES – TOURNAMENT-WISE

	M	I	No	Runs	HS	Ave	100	50	0	CT	B	M	Runs	Wkt	Ave	5s	10s	B/B	Captaincy			
																			W	L	Dr	To
Tests	37	57	6	1,775	169	34.80	3	10	6	31	853	12	501	9	55.67	0	0	2/9	0	0	0	0
Ranji Trophy	33	52	2	2,099	149	41.98	5	12	7	31	666	22	318	8	39.75	0	0	3/25	0	0	1	1
Duleep Trophy	9	16	3	1,151	209	88.54	6	3	0	11	12	1	1	0	0	0	0	–	0	0	0	0
Irani Cup	3	6	1	316	204 *	63.20	1	1	0	4	60	3	31	0	0	0	0	–	1	0	0	1
Other First-Class Matches	17	27	6	839	118	39.95	3	5	1	17	552	11	378	4	94.50	0	0	1/8	0	0	0	0
	99	**158**	**18**	**6180**	**209**	**44.14**	**18**	**31**	**14**	**94**	**2143**	**49**	**1229**	**21**	**58.52**	**0**	**0**	**3/25**	**1**	**0**	**1**	**2**

LIMITED-OVERS INTERNATIONAL MATCHES

ONE-DAY INTERNATIONALS

(debut v Kenya at Gymkhana Club Ground, Nairobi on 03-10-2000)

Season	M	I	No	Runs	HS	Ave	100	50	0	CT	B	M	Runs	Wkt	Ave	5s	10s	B/B	Captaincy			
																			W	L	Dr	To
2000–01 to 2011	274	252	38	8,051	139	37.62	13	49	14	84	4832	18	4060	109	37.25	1	0	5/31				

Highest score in ODIs: 139 v Australia at Sydney Cricket Ground, Sydney on 22-01-2004

Best bowling in ODIs: 531 v Ireland at M. Chinnaswamy Stadium, Bengaluru on 06-03-2011 in the World Cup

He was hit for a six off five balls of his over 0, 6, 6, 6, 6, 6 = 30 runs from his over – by A.D. Mascarenhas of England at the Oval on 05-09-2007

He was hit for most runs off the last over of the match. It was the 50th over of the innings, in which 30 runs were scored – A world record of most runs in the last over of the match.

TWENTY20 INTERNATIONALS

(debut v Scotland at Kingsmead, Durban on 13-09-2007 in the World Cup of 2007 in South Africa)

Season	M	I	No	Runs	H S	Ave	100	50	0	CT	B	M	Runs	Wkt	Ave	5s	10s	B/B	Captaincy			
																			W	L	Dr	To
2007 to 2012–13	29	27	5	667	70	30.32	0	5		8	228		289	16	18.06	0	0	3/23				

Highest score: 70 v Australia at Kingsmead, Durban on 22-09-2007 (World Cup Semi Final)

Best bowling: 3/23 v Sri Lanka at Mohali on 09-12-2009

Fastest Half Century: 50 in 12 balls with 3 x 4s and 6 x 6s v England at Kingsmead, Durban on 19-09-2007 (World Cup). His 58 came off 16 balls, with 3 x 4s and 7 x 6s.

He hit all six balls from Stuart Broad of England for a six, scoring 36 runs from a six-ball over, at Kingsmead, Durban on 19-09-2007 (World Cup)

YUVRAJ SINGH – 100s

	Scores	Opponent	Venue	Season
Tests (3)				
	112	Pakistan (2nd Test)	Gaddafi Stadium, Lahore	2003–04
	122	Pakistan (3rd Test)	National Stadium, Karachi	2005–06
	169	Pakistan (3rd Test)	M. Chinnaswamy Stadium, Bengaluru	2007–08
Ranji Trophy (5)				
	149	Haryana	Nehru Stadium, Gurgaon	1999–00
	135	Mumbai	Wankhede Stadium, Mumbai	2000–01
	109	Haryana	Tata Energy Research Institute, Oval, Gurgaon	2001–02
	102	Delhi	Gandhi Sports Complex Ground, Amritsar	2001–02
	138	Delhi	Punjab Cricket Association Stadium, Mohali	2003–04
Duleep Trophy (6)				
	130	Central Zone	Pherozshah Kotla Stadium, Delhi	2000–01

116

YUVRAJ SINGH – 100s

	Scores	Opponent	Venue	Season
	209	South Zone	Nahar Singh Stadium, Faridabad	2001–02
	106 & 148	East Zone	Punjab Cricket Association Stadium, Mohali	2003–04
	100 *	West Zone	K.D. Singh Babu Stadium, Lucknow	2004–05
	110	South Zone	Holkar Stadium, Indore	2004–05
Irani Cup (1)				
	204 *	For Rest of India v Mumbai	Sawai Mansingh Stadium, Jaipur	2010–11
Other First-class Cricket Matches (3)				
	107	For India 'A'	v South Africa 'A' at Bloemfontein	2001–02
	113	For Board President's XI	v Australia at Hyderabad	2008–09
	118	For Indians in Sri Lanka	v Sri Lanka Board President's XI at Colombo (Colts)	2010

YUVRAJ SINGH – 100s

	Scores	Opponent	Venue	Season
Century in both innings – in Duleep Trophy				
	106 & 148	For North Zone v East Zone	Punjab Cricket Association Stadium, Mohali	2003–04

Scores	Details of 100s	Opponent/Venue	Season
One-Day Internationals (13)			
102 *	85 balls, 9 x 4s, 4 x 6s	v Bangladesh at Dhaka	11-04-2003
139	122 balls, 16 x 4s, 2 x 6s	v Australia at Sydney	22-01-2004
110	114 balls, 11 x 4s, 1 x 6	v West Indies at Colombo (RPS)	07-08-2005
120	124 balls, 12 x 4s, 1 x 6	v Zimbabwe at Harare	04-09-2005

YUVRAJ SINGH – 100s

Scores	Details of 100s	Opponent/Venue	Season
103	122 balls, 10 x 4s, 3 x 6s	v South Africa at Hyderabad	16-11-2005
107 *	93 balls, 14 x 4s	v Pakistan at Karachi	18-02-2006
103	76 balls, 10 x 4s, 3 x 6s	v England at Margao	03-04-2006
121	115 balls, 12 x 4s, 3 x 6s	v Australia at Hyderabad	05-10-2007
138 *	78 balls, 16 x 4s, 6 x 6s	v England at Rajkot	14-11-2008
118	122 balls, 15 x 4s, 2 x 6s	v England at Indore	17-11-2008
117	95 balls, 17 x 4s, 1 x 6	v Sri Lanka at Colombo (RPS)	03-02-2009
131	102 balls, 10 x 4s, 7 x 6s	v West Indies at Kingston	26-06-2009
113	123 balls, 10 x 4s, 2 x 6s	v West Indies at Chennai (World Cup)	20-03-2011

Fast 100s

Scores	Details of 100s	Opponent/Venue	Season
Fast Centuries – in less than 100 balls			
100 in 64 balls	138 * in 78 balls, 16 x 4s, 6 x 6s	v England at Rajkot	14-11-2008
100 in 73 balls	103 in 76 balls, 10 x 4s, 3 x 6s	v England at Margao	03-04-2006
100 in 82 balls	117 in 95 balls, 17 x 4s, 1 x 6	v Sri Lanka at Colombo (RPS)	03-02-2009
100 in 85 balls	102 * in 85 balls, 9 x 4s, 4 x 6s	v Bangladesh at Dhaka	11-04-2003
100 in 88 balls	131 in 102 balls, 10 x 4s, 7 x 6s	v West Indies at Kingston	26-06-2009
100 in 99 balls	107 * in 93 balls, 14 x 4s	v Pakistan at Karachi	18-02-2006

Century Partnerships

Scores	Opponent/Venue	Season
Tests		
4th wicket		
172 runs with V.V.S Laxman	v Zimbabwe at Bulawayo	2005–06
128 with R.S. Dravid	v England at Nottingham	2011
5th wicket		
300 with S.C. Ganguly	v Pakistan at Bengaluru	2007–08
163 n o with S.R. Tendulkar	v England at Chennai	2008–09
153 with G. Gambhir	v England at Mohali	2008–09
125 with R.S. Dravid	v Sri Lanka at Ahmedabad	2009–10
120 n o with V.V.S. Laxman	v New Zealand at Napier	2008–09
110 with S.R. Tendulkar	v Pakistan at Multan	2003–04
103 with S.C. Ganguly	v Pakistan at Karachi	2005–06
102 with V.V.S. Laxman	v Sri Lanka at Kanpur	2009–10
7th wicket		
104 n o with M.S. Dhoni	v Sri Lanka at Delhi	2005–06

Century Partnerships

Scores	Opponent/Venue	Season
Century Partnerships – One-Day Internationals		
3rd wicket		
221 with V. Sehwag	v Sri Lanka at Colombo (RPS)	03-02-2009
146 * with M.S. Dhoni	v Pakistan at Karachi	18-02-2006
138 with S.R. Tendulkar	v New Zealand at Christchurch	08-03-2009
137 with V. Kohli	v Australia at Visakhapatnam	20-10-2010
135 with K.K.D. Karthik	v West Indies at Kingston	26-06-2009
122 with V. Kohli	v West Indies at Chennai	20-03-2011
118 with R.S. Dravid	v Pakistan at Rawalpindi	11-02-2006
115 with S.K. Raina	v England at Indore	15-04-2006
4th wicket		
213 with V.V.S. Laxman	v Australia at Sydney	22-01-2004
165 with Mohammad Kaif	v West Indies at Colombo (RPS)	07-08-2005
148 with M.S. Dhoni	v Australia at Delhi	31-10-2009

122

Century Partnerships

Scores	Opponent/Venue	Season
145 * with S.C. Ganguly	v Sri Lanka at Visakhapatnam	17-02-2007
134 with G. Gambhir	v England at Indore	17-11-2008
114 with R.S. Dravid	v England at Brisbane	20-01-2004
105 * with Mohammad Kaif	v Sri Lanka at Rajkot	09-11-2005
105 with S.R. Tendulkar	v Pakistan at Lahore	13-02-2006
105 with M.S. Dhoni	v Pakistan at Guwahati	05-11-2007
100 with M.S. Dhoni	v Pakistan at Kanpur	11-11-2007
5th wicket		
158 with D.B. Mongia	v Zimbabwe at Guwahati	19-03-2002
142 with S.K. Raina	v England at Margao	03-03-2006
133 with R.S. Dravid	v Sri Lanka at Dambulla	18-03-2004
122 with S.R. Tendulkar	v Bermuda at Port of Spain	19-03-2007
118 * with R.S. Dravid	v Kenya at Cape Town	07-03-2003
112 with M.S. Dhoni	v Pakistan at Karachi	02-07-2008

Century Partnerships

Scores	Opponent/Venue	Season
105 with M.S. Dhoni	v England at Rajkot	14-11-2008
103 with M.S. Dhoni	v Zimbabwe at Harare	29-08-2005
102 with R.S. Dravid	v Sri Lanka at Colombo	01-08-2001
101 with M.S. Dhoni	v Pakistan at Gwalior	15-11-2007
100 with M.S. Dhoni	v Pakistan at Gwalior	15-11-2007
6th wicket		
158 with M.S. Dhoni	v Zimbabwe at Harare	04-09-2005
121 with Mohammad Kaif	v England at Lord's	13-07-2002
102 * with M.S. Dhoni	v Pakistan at Lahore	13-02-2006

Tours Abroad

	Opponent		Season
For Tests	Pakistan		2002–03
	Zimbabwe		2005–06
	Pakistan		2005–06
	West Indies		2005–06
	Australia		2007–08
	New Zealand		2008–09
	Bangladesh		2009–10
	Sri Lanka		2010
	England		2011
	West Indies		2011–12
INDIA 'A'	South Africa	Toured as a replacement for Dinesh Mongia	2001–02

Tours Abroad

Opponent	Series/Venue	Season
For One-Day Internationals		
Kenya	ICC Knock-Out Tournament	October 2000
Sharjah	Champions Trophy	October 2000
Sri Lanka	3-nation series – India, New Zealand, Sri Lanka for Coca Cola Cup	July–August 2001
South Africa	Standard Bank Summer Spice Triangular series – India, Kenya, South Africa	October 2001
West Indies	5-match series	May–June 2002
England	3-nation series – England, India, Sri Lanka	July 2002
Sri Lanka	ICC Champions Trophy – Australia, Bangladesh, England, Holland, India, Kenya, New Zealand, Pakistan, South Africa, Sri Lanka, West Indies, Zimbabwe	September 2002
New Zealand	7-match series	January 2003

126

Tours Abroad

Opponent	Series/Venue	Season
South Africa, Zimbabwe, Kenya	ICC World Cup – Australia, Bangladesh, Canada, England, Holland, India, Kenya, Namibia, New Zealand, Pakistan, South Africa, Sri Lanka, West Indies, Zimbabwe	February–March 2003
Bangladesh	TVS Cup – Bangladesh, India, South Africa	April 2003
Australia	VB Series – Australia, India, Zimbabwe	January–February 2004
Pakistan	5-match series	March 2004
Sri Lanka	Asia Cup – Bangladesh, Hong Kong, India, Pakistan, Sri Lanka, UAE	July–August 2004
Holland	3-nation series – Australia, India, Pakistan	August 2004
England	Natwest Challenge	September 2004

Tours Abroad

Opponent	Series/Venue	Season
England	ICC Champions Trophy – Australia, Bangladesh, England, India, Kenya, New Zealand, Pakistan, South Africa, Sri Lanka, USA, West Indies, Zimbabwe	September 2004
Bangladesh	3-match series	December 2004
Sri Lanka	3-nation series – India, Sri Lanka, West Indies	August 2005
Zimbabwe	3-nation series – India, New Zealand, Zimbabwe	August–September 2005
Pakistan	5-match series	February 2006
Abu Dhabi, UAE	DLF Cup 2-match series v Pakistan	April 2006
West Indies	5-match series	May 2006
Sri Lanka	Tri-nation series – India, South Africa, Sri Lanka	August 2006
Malaysia	3-nation series – Australia, India, West Indies	September 2006

Tours Abroad

Opponent	Series/Venue	Season
West Indies	ICC World Cup – Australia, Bangladesh, Bermuda, Canada, England, Holland, India, Ireland, Kenya, New Zealand, Pakistan, Scotland, South Africa, Sri Lanka, West Indies, Zimbabwe	April 2007
Bangladesh	3-match series	May 2007
Ireland	One-off series v Ireland	June–July 2007
Scotland	Future Cup v South Africa	July 2007
Scotland	One-off series v Pakistan (Washed out totally)	July 2007
Scotland	One-off series	August 2007
England	7-match series	August–September 2007
Australia	Commonwealth Bank Trophy – Australia, India, Sri Lanka	February–March 2008

Tours Abroad

Opponent	Series/Venue	Season
Bangladesh	Kitply Cup – Bangladesh, India, Pakistan	June 2008
Pakistan	Asia Cup – Bangladesh, Hong Kong, India, Pakistan, Sri Lanka, UAE	June–July 2008
Sri Lanka	5-match series	August 2008
Sri Lanka	5-match series	January–February 2009
New Zealand	5-match series	March 2009
West Indies	4-match series	June 2009
Sri Lanka	Compac Cup 3-nation series – India, New Zealand, Sri Lanka	September 2009
Bangladesh	Tri-nation series – Bangladesh, India, Sri Lanka	January 2010
Sri Lanka	Triangular series – India, New Zealand, Sri Lanka	August 2010
South Africa	5-match series	January 2011

Tours Abroad

Opponent	Series/Venue	Season
TWENTY20		
South Africa	ICC World Cup	2007
England	ICC World Cup	2009
West Indies	ICC World Cup	2010
Sri Lanka	ICC World Cup	2012–13

YUVRAJ SINGH – Player of the Match

Sr No	Date	Venue	Rival teams/ Toss won by	Totals/overs	Rival skippers	Result
			ONE-DAY INTERNATIONALS (26)			
1	07-10-2000	Nairobi	India	265/9 off 50	S.C. Ganguly	India won by 20 runs
			Australia (T)	245 off 46.4	S.R. Waugh	
2	01-08-2001	Colombo (SSC)	India	227/8 off 50	S.C. Ganguly	India won by 46 runs
			Sri Lanka (T)	181 off 45.5	S.T. Jayasuriya	
3	16-03-2002	Hyderabad	Zimbabwe (T)	240/8 off 50	S.V. Carlisle	India won by 5 wkts
			India	244/5 off 48.1	S.C. Ganguly	
4	29-06-2002	Lord's	England (T)	271/7 off 50	Nasser Hussain	India won by 6 wkts
			India	272/4 off 48.5	S.C. Ganguly	
5	11-04-2003	Dhaka	India (T)	276 off 49.3	S.C. Ganguly	India won by 200 runs

YUVRAJ SINGH – Player of the Match

Sr No	Date	Venue	Rival teams/ Toss won by	Totals/overs	Rival skippers	Result
			Bangladesh	76 off 27.3	Khaled Mahmud	
6	20-01-2004	Brisbane	India (T)	255/6 off 50	S.C. Ganguly	India won by 24 runs
			Zimbabwe	231 off 47.1	H.H. Streak	
7	22-01-2004	Sydney	India (T)	296/4 off 50	S.C. Ganguly	Aus won by 2 wkts (D/L)
			Australia	225/8 off 33.5	R.T. Ponting	
8	07-08-2005	Colombo (RPS)	India (T)	262/4 off 50	R.S. Dravid	India won by 7 runs
			West Indies	255/9 off 50	S.C. Joseph	
9	04-09-2005	Harare	Zimbabwe	250 off 50	T. Taibu	India won by 4 wkts
			India (T)	255/6 off 48.1	S.C. Ganguly	
10	16-11-2005	Hyderabad	India	249/9 off 50	R.S. Dravid	S A won by 5 wkts

133

Sr No	Date	Venue	Rival teams/ Toss won by	Totals/overs	Rival skippers	Result
			South Africa (T)	252/5 off 48.5	G.C. Smith	
11	18-02-2006	Karachi	Pakistan	286/8 off 50	Inzamamul Haq	India won by 8 wkts
			India (T)	287/2 off 46.5	R.S. Dravid	
12	03-04-2006	Margao	India (T)	294/6 off 50	R.S. Dravid	India won by 49 runs
			England	245 off 48.5	A. Flintoff	
13	06-04-2006	Kochi	England (T)	237 off 48.4	A. Flintoff	India won by 4 wkts
			India	238/6 off 47.2	R.S. Dravid	
14	01-07-2007	Belfast	South Africa	148/7 off 31	J.H. Kallis	India won by 6 wkts
			India (T)	152/4 off 30.2	R.S. Dravid	
15	11-11-2007	Kanpur	India	294/6 off 50	M.S. Dhoni	India won by 46 runs

YUVRAJ SINGH – Player of the Match

YUVRAJ SINGH – Player of the Match

Sr No	Date	Venue	Rival teams/ Toss won by	Totals/overs	Rival skippers	Result
			Pakistan (T)	248 off 47.2	Shoaib Malik	
16	14-11-2008	Rajkot	India	387/5 off 50	M.S. Dhoni	India won by 158 runs
			England (T)	229 off 37.4	K.P. Pietersen	
17	17-11-2008	Indore	India (T)	292/9 off 50	M.S. Dhoni	India won by 54 runs
			England	238 off 47	K.P. Pietersen	
18	30-02-2009	Colombo (RPS)	India (T)	363/5 off 50	M.S. Dhoni	India won by 147 runs
			Sri Lanka	216 off 41.4	D.P.M.D. Jayawardene	
19	08-02-2009	Colombo (RPS)	Sri Lanka (T)	320/8 off 50	D.P.M.D. Jayawardene	S L won by 68 runs
			India	252 off 48.5	M.S. Dhoni	
20	26-06-2009	Kingston	India (T)	339/6 off 50	M.S. Dhoni	India won by 20 runs
			West Indies	319 off 48.1	C.H. Gayle	

135

Sr No	Date	Venue	Rival teams/ Toss won by	Totals/overs	Rival skippers	Result
			YUVRAJ SINGH – Player of the Match			
21	31-10-2009	Delhi	Australia (T)	229/5 off 50	R.T. Ponting	India won by 6 wkts
			India	230/4 off 48.2	M.S. Dhoni	
22	10-12-2010	Chennai	New Zealand (T)	103 off 27	D.L. Vettori	India won by 8 wkts
			India	107/2 of f 21.1	M.S. Dhoni	
23	06-03-2011 (World Cup)	Bengaluru	Ireland	207 off 47.5	W.T.S. Porterfield	India won by 5 wkts
			India (T)	210/5 off 46	M.S. Dhoni	
24	09-03-2011 (World Cup)	Delhi	Netherlands (T)	189 off 46.4	P.W. Borren	India won by 5 wkts
			India	191/5 off 36.3	M.S. Dhoni	
25	20-03-2011 (World Cup)	Chennai	India (T)	268 off 49.1	M.S. Dhoni	India won by 80 runs
			West Indies	188 off 43	D.J.G. Sammy	
26	24-03-2011 (World Cup Quarter Final)	Ahmedabad	Australia (T)	260/6 off 50	R.T. Ponting	India won by 5 wkts

YUVRAJ SINGH – Player of the Match

Sr No	Date	Venue	Rival teams/ Toss won by	Totals/overs	Rival skippers	Result
			India	261/5 off 47.4	M.S. Dhoni	
	02-04-2011 (World Cup Final)	Mumbai (Wankhede)	Sri Lanka (T)	274/6 off 50	K.C. Sangakkara	India won by 6 wkts
			India	277/4 off 48.2	M.S. Dhoni	

After the conclusion of the final in Mumbai, Yuvraj Singh was declared Player of the World Cup 2011 in Bangladesh, India and Sri Lanka. He had already won the Player of the Match Awards in four World Cup matches earlier in the tournament. He aggregated 362 runs at the average of 90.50 and bagged 15 wickets conceding 25.13 runs apiece in a total of 9 matches, with 5 for 31 as his best bowling against Ireland at Bengaluru on 6 March 2011. His all round performance in the match comprised of 5 for 31 and an unbeaten 50.

TWENTY20 INTERNATIONALS (4)

Sr No	Date	Venue	Rival teams/ Toss won by	Totals/overs	Rival skippers	Result
1	19-09-2007 (World Cup)	Durban	India (T)	218/4 off 20	M.S. Dhoni	India won by 18 runs
			England	200/6 off 20	P.D. Collingwood	

YUVRAJ SINGH – Player of the Match

Sr No	Date	Venue	Rival teams/ Toss won by	Totals/overs	Rival skippers	Result
2	22-09-2007 (World Cup)	Durban	India (T)	188/5 off 20	M.S. Dhoni	India won by 15 runs
			Australia	173/7 off 20	A.C. Gilchrist	
3	12-12-2009	Mohali	Sri Lanka (T)	206/7 off 20	K.C. Sangakkara	India won by 6 wickets
			India	211/4 off 19.1	M.S. Dhoni	
4	02-10-2012 (World Cup)	Colombo (RPS)	India	152/6 off 20	M.S. Dhoni	India won by 1 run
			South Africa (T)	151 off 19.5	A.B. de Villiers	

CAREER HIGHLIGHTS

- Born on 12 December 1981 in Chandigarh
- Left-handed middle-order batsman and left-arm slow spinner
- Son of Test cricketer Yograj Singh (India Test cap No. 152)

FIRST-CLASS CRICKET

- Played Ranji Trophy as an opener for Punjab against Orissa at Punjab Cricket Association Stadium in Mohali, 7–10 February 1997, in Super League Group A and was dismissed on 0.
- He made his first-class cricket debut at his age of 16 years and 57 days when he represented Punjab in the Ranji Trophy at Mohali, 7 February 1997.
- His career best knock came in Duleep Trophy when, playing for North Zone he scored 209 against South Zone at Nahar Singh Stadium at Faridabad in 2001–02.
- His other double century – 204 not out, was hit in the Irani Cup fixture at Sawai Mansingh Stadium in Jaipur in 2010–11. His 204 came in 302 min, 194 balls, with 28 x 4s and 5 x 6s. His first 100 came in 121 balls, with 17 x 4s and the next one in 192 balls, 28 x 4s and 5 x 6s

- He holds the distinction of scoring a century in both innings of a Duleep Trophy match for North Zone against East Zone at Punjab Cricket Association Stadium in Mohali in 2003–04.
- He played his first first-class cricket match (Ranji Trophy) at Punjab Cricket Association Stadium in Mohali, 7 February 1997 and at this very Stadium, he also played his first Test v New Zealand on 16 October 2003.
- All of his three centuries in Tests were hit against Pakistan – two in Pakistan and one in India. His career highest score of 169 was hit at M. Chinnaswamy Stadium in Bengaluru in 2007–08.
- He participated in the County Cricket Championship in England, playing for Yorkshire in 2003 for 145 runs at the average of 14.50 with two half centuries in seven matches.

TESTS

- He earned India Test cap No. 247 in the season 2003–04, when he made his debut in the second Test against New Zealand at Punjab Cricket Association Stadium in Mohali, 16–20 October 2003.

ONE-DAY INTERNATIONALS

- He made his debut in One-Day Internationals against Kenya at Gymkhana Club Ground in Nairobi on 03-10-2000.

- His 13 centuries in One-Day Internationals include six hundreds which were hit in less than 100 balls:

  1. In 64 balls, when he made 138 n o in 78 balls with 16 x 4s and 6 x 6s against England at Rajkot on 14-11-2008
  2. In 73 balls, when he made 103 in 76 balls, with 10 x 4s and 3 x 6s against England at Margao on 03-04-2008
  3. In 82 balls, when he made 117 in 95 balls, with 17 x 4s and 1 x 6 against Sri Lanka at R. Premadasa Stadium in Colombo on 03-02-2009
  4. In 85 balls, when he made 102 n o in 85 balls, with 9 x 4s and 4 x 6s against Bangladesh at Bangabandhu National Stadium in Dhaka on 11-04-2003
  5. In 88 balls, when he made 131 in 102 balls, with 10 x 4s and 7 x 6s against West Indies at Kingston on 26-06-2009
  6. In 99 balls, when he made 107 n o in 93 balls, with 14 x 4s against Pakistan at Karachi on 18-02-2006

- His best bowling figures of 5 wickets for 31 runs were against Ireland in the World Cup match at Bengaluru on 06-03-2011
- Five balls of his 6-ball over were hit for a six by England tail-end batsman Adrian Mascarenhas at the Oval on 05-09-2007. It was the last over of the match in which 30 runs were scored, which is a world record of most runs in the last over of the match.

141

- He earned the Player of the Tournament Award in the World Cup 2011 in Bangladesh, India and Sri Lanka, after playing 9 matches scoring therein 362 runs @ 90.50 and claiming 15 wickets @ 25.13 runs apiece, and also earning Player of the Match Award in four of the 9 matches of the World Cup.
- His all-round performance of a half century and 5 wickets in the same match is also one of the best all-round performances in the World Cup matches of 2011 – 50 n o and 5 wickets for 31 runs v Ireland at M. Chinnaswamy Stadium in Bengaluru on 06-03-2011 has been the best all-round display in the Tournament.

TWENTY20 INTERNATIONALS

- 70 is his highest score in the Twenty20 internationals made against Australia at Kingsmead in Durban on 22-09-2007 (World Cup)
- 3 for 23 is his best bowling in Twenty20 internationals – against Sri Lanka at Mohali on 09-12-2009
- He has to his credit, the record of the fastest half century in Twenty20 internationals – 50 in 12 balls with 3 x 4s and 6 x 6s in his knock of 58 (in 16 balls, with 3 x 4s and 7 x 6s) against England at Kingsmead, Durban on 19-09-2007 (World Cup)
- He holds the world record of hitting all six balls of an over for a six – off Stuart Broad of England, off whose six balls, he hit six sixes scoring 36 runs at Kingsmead,

Durban on 19-09-2007 in the World Cup of 2007 in South Africa.

- He played for Kings XI Punjab as their captain in 2008 (15 matches), 2009 (14 matches in South Africa), 2010 (14 matches) and for Pune Warriors India in 2011 (14 matches).
- He performed two hat-tricks in the IPL tournament of 2009 in South Africa:
  1. Playing for Kings XI Punjab, he claimed Royal Challengers' Robin Uthappa and Jacques Kallis off the 5th and 6th balls of the 11 over and and Mark Boucher off the 1st ball of the 13th over of the innings at Kingsmead, Durban on 01-05-2009.
  2. In another match against Deccan Chargers at Johannesburg on 17-05-2009, he claimed Herschelle Gibbs off the 6th ball of the 11th over and Andrew Symonds off the 1st ball and Venugopal Rao off 2nd ball of 13th over at New Wanderers Stadium in Johannesburg on 17-05-2009.